ENGAGED
LEARNING

ENGAGED LEARNING

Richard VanDeWeghe

Foreword by Richard Sterling

CORWIN
A SAGE Company

For information:

Corwin
A SAGE Company
2455 Teller Road
Thousand Oaks, California 91320
(800) 233-9936
Fax: (800) 417-2466
www.corwinpress.com

SAGE India Pvt. Ltd.
B 1/I 1 Mohan Cooperative
Industrial Area
Mathura Road, New Delhi 110 044
India

SAGE Ltd.
1 Oliver's Yard
55 City Road
London EC1Y 1SP
United Kingdom

SAGE Asia-Pacific Pte. Ltd.
33 Pekin Street #02-01
Far East Square
Singapore 048763

Printed in the United States of America.

Library of Congress Cataloging-in-Publication Data

VanDeWeghe, Richard.
Engaged learning/Richard VanDeWeghe.
     p. cm.
Includes bibliographical references and index.
ISBN 978-1-4129-6628-3 (cloth)
ISBN 978-1-4129-6629-0 (pbk.)
    1. Motivation in education. 2. Learning, Psychology of. 3. Reflective teaching. I. Title.

LB1065.V265 2009
370.15'4—dc22   2008044767

This book is printed on acid-free paper.

09   10   11   12   13   10   9   8   7   6   5   4   3   2   1

Acquisitions Editor:	Hudson Perigo
Editorial Assistant:	Lesley K. Blake
Production Editor:	Libby Larson
Copy Editor:	Jenifer Dill
Typesetter:	C&M Digitals (P) Ltd.
Proofreader:	Wendy Jo Dymond
Indexer:	Terri Corry
Cover Designer:	Karine Hovsepian

Contents

Foreword

Teachers live in a dynamic, fast-changing world. New students arrive every year, and teachers must respond to the young people walking in the door. The most effective teachers are always asking questions about what works, what they can learn from the research in their discipline, and what they can learn from their colleagues.

One may start by identifying the underlying complexities that are in fact the very basic needs that apply to all students. Will they be able to meet the literacy demands—reading, writing, listening, and speaking—expected of them? Will they want to participate fully in learning activities that will enable them to reach their potential? For answers to these questions, teachers must not only turn to their own discipline but must also reach across many fields, including language studies, sociology, and psychology, and try to make a coherent plan for themselves. Those of us in networks, like the National Writing Project, frequently turn to our colleagues to make sense of these contexts, but it is a great deal of work for any one person to do, particularly when each school day demands so much.

For these reasons, it was with great anticipation that I turned to Professor VanDeWeghe's new book *Engaged Learning.* How, I wondered, can VanDeWeghe combine what we know about language learning, the demands of a subject discipline, the demands of learning to read and write about complex material, and the demand to conduct classroom-based research with what we know about a human being's natural inclination to learn, collaborate, and make new knowledge his or her own?

Engaged Learning thoughtfully addresses all of these issues. Throughout the book, VanDeWeghe illustrates his points with narratives and provides classroom examples in a skillful before-and-after format, consistently reinforcing the basic principles of engagement that lead to powerful learning. Using Csikszentmihalyi's theories of flow as a baseline goal, he uses engagement as the engine that drives learning activities. Thus, engaging "brains" and "hearts" to achieve flow becomes the goal, and applying engagement to instruction, assessment, and the curriculum become the methods. Of course, powerful teaching, engaging curriculum, and effective assessment must by necessity make use of what we know about how people learn, and so *Engaged Learning* circles back to the social nature of learning, the power of collaboration, and the delicate balance of power between teacher and students. VanDeWeghe also delves into the ways that young people develop arguments and the basis for their reasoning. He then describes a path, a personal journey if you will, that he suggests young people need to embark upon in order to break away from reductive, dichotomized thinking.

Although *Engaged Learning* advocates for learners' autonomy and knowledge, VanDeWeghe also acknowledges that the demands made on teachers to create an enabling environment are not small. He calls on teachers to read and understand learning in a way that may be unfamiliar, just as developing metacognitive skills in students will be largely unfamiliar to them.

Engagement is a subject of much discussion among educators everywhere. Often, talk among teachers turns to how teenagers and other young people spend their time outside of school, the level of commitment they bring to those activities, and an often invidious comparison with the level of engagement in their classrooms. Young people are enormously engaged in the day-to-day lives of their peers and their own personal interests outside of school. We have seen a veritable explosion of young people's involvement in computer gaming, the creation of Web content, and various forms of written communication between and among their friends. How then to capture that engagement for the classroom? This book describes processes that help to negotiate these barriers.

Engaged Learning shows the way forward to necessary changes for all students to find powerful learning in their school lives. The literacy practices advocated here, the strategies set out in such detail, will enable teachers of every subject and discipline to redefine their teaching across the entire curriculum. The book plumbs the depths of engagement in every aspect and place in education. No classroom process, whether it is reading out loud or listening and discussing, or re-creating historical events or conducting science experiments, is left unexamined. VanDeWeghe's *Engaged Learning* identifies the principles and practices for the classroom that may well recapture the energy and enthusiasm that young people pour into the activities they love.

The classrooms that may result from a diligent use of this book will look very different from the usual, and in some cases, its use could collide head on with current understandings of what constitutes learning and achievement. But imagine a classroom in which 30 or more students are actively engaged in learning, both with their hearts and minds! Isn't it time that such schools were available to all?

—Richard Sterling

Preface

I have been a teacher for more than four decades. In all these years of teaching, mentoring, administering, and collaborating with very smart educators, I have come to believe that although teachers may appear to be separated by grade levels or subject matter, they are not separated when it comes to wanting classrooms teeming with actively engaged learners.

This book began, and continues, as an inquiry into engaged learning. All my teaching life, I've tried to get students deeply invested in learning. Many times, they seem engaged and motivated—even show it—and many times they do not. Most often, their level of engagement seems to be somewhere in between. I always wondered what makes a class go well or not so well. I also wondered what happens to students cognitively and emotionally when they get genuinely involved in learning. Mainly, I wondered, How can I be a better teacher?

Then something happened that started me thinking more deeply and systematically about the nature of engaged learning. The University of Colorado Denver, where I teach English, had a faculty teaching-mentoring program, and I mentored an assistant professor of psychology who was in his second year. I visited John's statistics class many times that semester as an observer and coach, and we debriefed after each visit. I wanted to know more about statistics anyway, and so I looked forward to learning more through the mentoring experience. His class met in a small amphitheatre-style classroom: professor in front, 30 students sitting at tables that swooped around the room in a semicircle, with each row on a riser.

On one particular day, John lectured on standard error of measurement. I sat in the back row, toward the left side of the room; about six or seven students filled the other seats in my row. I had a good view of most students in the room. John spoke from notes, frequently using the whiteboard and the overhead projector to illustrate points. About halfway through the class, I noticed that many of the students were barely paying attention to John's lecture; it was pretty dry stuff. In my row, a few students were doodling. The woman in front of me was either taking notes in iambic trimeter or actually writing a poem. From John's vantage point, he could only see that they were writing in their notebooks, so to him, they appeared to be paying attention.

Then, the unusual happened. John paused in midlecture, gazed out the window as if in a reverie, turned to the class, and said, "You know, this point about error reminds me of last weekend. I was in Ohio attending my high school class reunion and the funniest thing took place. . . ." He then told an entertaining anecdote that illustrated the lecture point he had been presenting. The story involved some latent interpersonal rivalry that had never been resolved: a date gone awry, with two guys still holding strong feelings about who did what. What captured my attention were the students in my row. As John told his story, they abandoned their doodles and they listened. They chuckled at the humor in the story and, I'm guessing, probably remembered that story and how it connected with the lecture. I was sure, however, that John's spontaneous narrative engaged the entire class, even the statistics poet sitting in front of me. There was physical evidence that he had captured their attention: I could see it right before my eyes. Sadly, however, after John told his story and returned to the lecture, students in the back row went back to doodling.

After class, John and I went for coffee. When I told him how the level of attention took a dramatic turn when he told the story, he was surprised. "I didn't plan that," he said. "The reunion was just last weekend and still in the back of my mind. Somehow it seemed relevant to my lecture and so I threw it in. I don't do that sort of thing very often. You know, tell stories."

I said, "You ought to."

"What? Tell stories?"

"You bet. That was a good one. And if what I saw today is any indication, when you tell stories *and* lecture, your students pay more attention."

John laughed. "I do statistics. I don't do stories. I'm not a storyteller."

I said, "Storytellers are people who tell stories. Looks like you're a storyteller. That's what you did and look what happened. If I were you, especially when teaching something like statistics, I'd tell a lot of stories. I would plan stories to go with lessons, just as you did today."

John sat back, his eyes narrowed. "I didn't plan it," he said. "It just sort of came out. Besides, I haven't had any experiences that would fit other lessons."

"So what?" I said. "Make them up. Make up characters, events, mysteries, anything that would serve to illustrate the lecture points!"

So he did. In fact, he had one ready for the very next class. Then he made up a host of stories to go along with his other lectures. As he integrated more narratives, he watched the students' reactions. He told me that he thought more students paid more attention when he told stories, and he thought teaching that particular class was becoming more interesting too. I suspect students learned more, but the class wasn't a controlled research study so we couldn't be sure (though common sense, brain research, and years of teaching tell me that when people pay better attention, they learn more). Something happened in those students' brains. Something happened in John's too. And something happened in mine.

This event got me thinking—and wondering—about the power of brain-based teaching. *Before* he began telling stories, John's lectures were based on a mode of thought and speaking that Jerome Bruner (1986) calls *paradigmatic*, that is, a "formal . . . system of description and explanation" that employs "categorization or conceptualization" (p. 14). Such expository ways of teaching are most common in all levels of schooling, where teachers need to "cover the material." But when he told his story, he appealed to another mode of thought, what Bruner calls *narrative*, or story. In brain research terms, John switched "memory pathways," from *semantic* (i.e., word based) pathways to *episodic* (e.g., vignette) pathways. Using two modes of thought rather than one appealed to two memory pathways—and to his students as they became more engaged learners. I'll have more to say about memory pathways later.

Besides thinking more about brains and learning, I also began wondering if *humanistic theory* about learning might complement brain science. When John connected his "little story" (the reunion) to the "big story" concept (standard error of measurement), he helped students think deeper about how the real lives of real people and a statistical measurement are related. In *humanizing* the subject matter, he connected with his students, as all good teachers do at times, in a way that seemed so natural: As he said, the story "just sort of came out." As a literacy researcher, I had observed that brain science and humanistic theory were seldom linked with one another. There were those who expressed much excitement about what research on the brain would tell us about learning, and there were those theorists and thinkers whose excitement stemmed from their conviction that true learning springs from matters of the heart. In my mind, however, engaged learning is both brain *and* heart based. Many books about teaching consider *either* brain-based *or* humanistically based approaches to teaching but not both together. Such either-or thinking inhibits us from understanding the comprehensive way uniting both perspectives furthers learning. Separating brain and heart reminds me of the dissociation of the "two cultures" (science and the humanities) that C. P. Snow (1998) warns about: "It is dangerous to have two cultures that can't or don't communicate" (p. 98).

Mind- and heart-based engagement is a *way of thinking* about practice, a metaphorical lens I discuss as *wholesight,* a term employed by Parker

Palmer (1993) to unite mind and heart, just as Snow (1998) urges us to attend to *both* science *and* the humanities. When we look at teaching practices through this lens, we focus on what makes for compelling learning in our classrooms. I believe that if we can develop wholesight, our teaching will gain integrity, our decision making about practice will take on a heightened professionalism, and our students will learn better. To these ends, I hope the book will illuminate the following:

> What makes students excited about learning and, conversely, what makes them disaffected or only marginally involved?
>
> What do flow experiences have to teach us about the nature of engaged learning?
>
> How can we plan our teaching based on a deep understanding of student minds and hearts when they're truly engaged in learning?
>
> What do typical classroom activities such as reading and discussing look like when they are guided by mind- and heart-based engagement theory?

In this book, you will see examples taken primarily from English/language arts, science, math, social studies, and other subjects. You will read about elementary teachers and students as well as those in secondary and postsecondary schools. That breadth represents not only my background as a teacher and teacher educator but also my belief that engagement from brain- and heart-based perspectives encompasses learners of all ages and in all areas. I use fictitious names of teachers and students throughout the classroom vignettes presented here. These vignettes are either classes I've taught myself, classroom events I've witnessed or had described to me, or scenes and interviews that I have reconstructed through field notes. In Part II, I take some liberty by suggesting ways that a classroom could have been improved rather than what actually did happen or what may have happened.

In anticipation of the skeptical reader, a few things should be discussed up front. First, I do not explore the research on bodies in engaged states, though I know full well that engagement does include human bodies, especially in what is known as "mind-body states," as I discuss. Kinesthetic learning—the relation between body and brain—is vital to the ways many people learn, as it is one of the *multiple intelligences*. I do not ignore the body here; I just don't go into the detail that would be needed in order to present an intellectually respectable discussion of its role in engagement.

In addition, brain research indicates differences in brain structure and activity between males and females (Gurian, Henley, & Trueman, 2001; Gurian & Stevens, 2004). This research shows that many of the gender-based challenges we face in the classroom are, in fact, based on neurological differences between the sexes. Specific gender-based practices, while not the focus of this book, are nonetheless compatible with the broader applications I discuss. That is, here I identify brain- and heart-based practices as *natural* ways of learning; similarly, gender-based brain researchers recommend *nature-based* approaches "to call attention to the importance of basing . . . education strategies on a research-driven biological understanding of human learning" (Gurian & Stevens, 2004, p. 24).

I do not address the challenges of engagement for students with significant learning disabilities or who are English language learners. While there is no doubt in my mind that the principles of brain- and heart-based engagement apply directly to these two populations, building their special needs into this theory would distract from my main purpose, which is to paint the broad strokes of engaged learning. I leave that for another time.

It is important to note, too, that many concepts appearing here could be presented in much greater detail. Certainly that is true of the neurological issues, such as synaptic formation and development, electrochemical activity, and emotions and cognition. The same is true of the humanistic concepts. Take mindfulness, for example, where I discuss it in terms familiar to most people. If we consider that concept solely from the perspective of Eastern philosophy, we discover that it has many layers of complexity. As Thich Nhat Hahn (1998) writes, in order for one to truly understand and practice mindfulness, one must master the "Seven Miracles of Mindfulness," the "Four Establishments of Mindfulness," and the many ways to practice mindfulness (pp. 59–73). It is my hope that the interested reader will build on the overview in this book and pursue such scientific issues and humanistic concepts in greater depth for a richer understanding of engagement.

As a teacher and a teacher educator, I've always believed that science, theory, and empirical research ought to support classroom practice. This book attempts to put all four together—to give both scientific and humanistic integrity to instructional practice that is supported by educational research. Part I presents the scientific and humanistic perspectives that derive from an understanding of flow experiences. Part II presents engaging instructional practices that have been proven effective by empirical studies. I believe that we are more powerful and more confident teachers when wholesight drives our teaching and consequently our students' learning. For the ultimate state of engagement, flow experiences unite mind and spirit—thinking and feeling—into mind-body states, as Alan Shapiro (2006) writes about his own writing life:

> We write . . . for the same reason we read or look at paintings or listen to music: for the total immersion of the experience, the narrowing and intensification of focus to the right here, right now, the deep joy of bringing the entire soul to bear upon a single act of concentration. It is self-forgetful even if you are writing about the self, because you yourself have disappeared into the pleasure of making: your identity—the incessant, transient, noisy New York Stock Exchange of desires and commitments, ambitions, hopes, hates, appetites, and interests—has been obliterated by the rapture of complete attentiveness. In that extended moment, opposites cohere: the mind feels and the heart thinks, and receptivity's a form of fierce activity. Quotidian distinctions between mind and body, self and other, space and time, dissolve. (p. 205)

Acknowledgments

Ever since I began teaching, my wife, Judy—best friend and teacher extraordinaire herself—has been part of the now-decades-long conversation that formed this book. Her wisdom about teaching, knowledge about classrooms, and empathy for learners has nurtured and grown my understanding of what it means to be an engaged learner. I have been privileged to love and be married to someone whose patience with my nearly intolerable writing moods taught me vital lessons about pace, life's priorities, and perspective. For her critical listening, her sharp questions, and her infinitely renewable encouragement, first thanks go to Judy.

I have the directors and teacher-writers of the Denver Writing Project to thank for proving over and over that honoring teachers' knowledge about teaching and learning gets the important work of the classroom done well. Thanks to them for teaching me to be ever more curious about teachers-as-writers and about teaching anything, but especially writing and reading. I have the National Writing Project to thank for welcoming me and hundreds of thousands of other teachers into a dynamic community of inquiring minds with insatiable appetites for creating new knowledge and for instilling integrity into teaching and teachers' lives.

Colleagues and fellow teachers at Michigan State University and the University of Colorado Denver have also influenced this book, as their thoughtful reflections on engagement gave rise to many of my own. At the CU Presidents' Teaching Scholars retreats some of the finest teachers in the university challenged and extended my thinking to the point where the drive home down the mountains was always a risky affair as my mind swam in ideas and the voice in my head replayed the provocative talks and presentations that filled the retreats.

But it is the students who have taught me the most about what it means to be an engaged learner. Whether those adolescent seventh graders in Battle Creek, the basic writers at New Mexico State University, or the thousands of undergraduate and graduate students at the University of Colorado Denver, I have them to thank for making me really listen, ask important questions, say "What if?" an awful lot, and make understanding good teaching a life quest.

Finally, the good people at Corwin have been wonderful allies and supporters. Special thanks to Hudson Perigo, executive editor, for her advocacy and advice throughout the writing of this book.

Corwin gratefully acknowledges the contributions of the following reviewers:

Debby Chessin, EdD
Associate Professor of Curriculum
  & Instruction
The University of Mississippi
University, MS

Kathleen Choma
Math Teacher
South Brunswick High School
South Brunswick, NJ

Sara Coleman
Chemistry Instructor
Norwalk High School
Norwalk, IA

Cindy Corlett
Middle School Science Teacher
Parker, CO

Elizabeth F. Day
Grade 6 Teacher
Mechanicville Middle School
Mechanicville, NY

April DeGennaro
Teacher of Gifted
Peeples Elementary,
Fayette County Schools
Fayetteville, GA

Jeremy Kennson Dove
Science Teacher, Curriculum Advisor
Monticello High School
Charlottesville, VA

Nancy Foote
Math Specialist
Higley Unified School District
Gilbert, AZ

Carol Gallegos
Literacy Coach
Hanford Elementary School District
Hanford, CA

Marta Ann Gardner
Literacy Coach
Los Angeles Unified School District
Los Angeles, CA

Christopher Harris
Assistant Professor
University of Arizona
Tucson, AZ

Katrina Ladopoulos
Teacher
Oregon, WI

Kristie Betts Letter
National Board Professional
  Teacher of English
Peak to Peak High School
Lafayette, CO

Edward C. Nolan
Mathematics Department Chair
Albert Einstein High School
Kensington, MD

Jennifer L. Palmer
Reading Specialist
Harford County Public Schools
Bel Air, MD

Patricia Palmer
Sixth Grade, NBCT
Wynford Schools
Bucyrus, OH

Renee Ponce-Nealon
Kindergarten Teacher/National
  Board Certified Teacher
McDowell Elementary School
Petaluma, CA

Ronald W. Poplau
Instructor & Director of Continuing
  Education for Ottawa University
Shawnee Mission Northwest
  High School and also Ottawa
  University
Shawnee, KS

Jonathan Potter
Adjunct Professor
University College at
Rockland (UMA)
Rockport, ME

Cynthia Rowell
Area Instructional Lead Teacher
Cobb County Public Schools
Marietta, GA

Emily Shoemaker, EdD
Professor of Education
University of La Verne
La Verne, CA

Mrs. Patti Ulshafer
First Grade Teacher
Wilson Borough Elementary
  School
Easton, PA

Julie Wakefield
Geography Teacher
McQueen High School
Reno, NV

Thea H. Williams-Black, PhD
Assistant Professor of Elementary
  Education
The University of Mississippi
Oxford, MS

About the Author

 **Richard VanDeWeghe** is associate professor of English at the University of Colorado Denver. He has taught middle school and high school, he has been a faculty member at two universities, and he is a Field Director for the National Writing Project. He has directed two sites of the National Writing Project, supervised preservice teachers in the Initial Professional Teacher Education program at the University of Colorado Denver, and worked with practicing teachers in numerous schools and districts on reading, writing, and thinking across the curriculum.

Richard has a bachelor's degree in English Education from Western Michigan University, a master of arts degree in English from Michigan State University, and a doctorate in English with a specialty in the teaching of writing from Michigan State. He has been awarded Teacher of the Year at the University of Colorado Denver, where he was also named a President's Teaching Scholar. He was selected as Outstanding Educational Leader (1992) by the Colorado Language Arts Society, and his teacher study group leadership resulted in the 2006 National Network for Educational Renewal, Richard C. Clark Partner School Award.

His research interests concern theoretical and empirical issues that inform instructional practice—engaged learning; reading, writing, and thinking across the curriculum; teacher education; teacher professional development through inquiry; and the intersection of brain research and humanistic education. He has published articles in such resources as *Educational Leadership*, *Phi Delta Kappan*, *English Education*, *English Journal*, and the *Journal of Teaching Writing*. He was writer and column editor of the "Research Matters" column for *English Journal* for six years. He has presented workshops and papers for the National Council of Teachers of English, the National Writing Project, College Composition and

Communication, the Modern Language Association, and the Australian Reading Association.

Richard lives in northern Michigan with his wife, Judy, and daughter, Sophie. He may be contacted by email at rick.vandeweghe@ucdenver.edu

PART I

Flow, Minds, and Hearts

When people seem driven to learn by some compelling force, when they find themselves totally enveloped in an exhilarating search for knowledge, answers, insight, or accomplishment, they are likely to encounter states of optimal experience that are intellectual, emotional, physical, spiritual, or any combination thereof. The term *flow* is used by psychologist Mihaly Csikszentmihalyi (1990a) to describe such moments

> when a person's body or mind is stretched to its limits in a voluntary effort to accomplish something difficult and worthwhile. For a child, it could be placing with trembling fingers the last block on a tower she has built, higher than any she has built so far; for a swimmer, it could be trying to beat his own record; for a violinist, mastering an intricate musical passage. For each person there are thousands of opportunities, challenges to expand our selves. (p. 3)

Each of the first three chapters in Part I lays part of the foundation for this perspective on engaged learning, but all should be understood as a whole, which I try to show in the fourth chapter.

Chapter 1, "Engagement as Flow," discusses the nature of flow activities, describing that state as researchers have presented it and as we ourselves have experienced it (and most of us have experienced it at one time or another). Readers, for instance, often experience moments of flow when they find themselves in the grip of a compelling book, as writer Natalie Goldberg (2000) describes while reading her first Louis L'Amour novel:

> I remember clearly and with awe the sensation of my mind that day. It was as though I'd hooked it up to a Concorde jet and was shooting across open space . . . that total obliteration I experienced scared me. The wipe-out was pure, complete; I was knocked unconscious, like unadulterated lust. I'm not a prude. I just prefer to be slammed awake—fully alive in the land and characters. I have respect for the experience, the total trance L'Amour put me in. (p. 120)

The most complete and all-encompassing state of engagement, flow is our ideal, our target as teachers. If we can better understand flow—how it comes about and how it is based on both brain and heart activity—then we have a better chance at selecting and revising teaching practices so that more engagement happens. If we can teach for engagement, our students will learn more, remember more, become more passionate about learning, and know in their minds and hearts the experience of genuinely engaged learning. Engagement is the key to a lifelong love of learning.

I present a continuum in Chapter 1 that depicts a range of engaged learning, from totally unengaged to fully engaged (flow state):

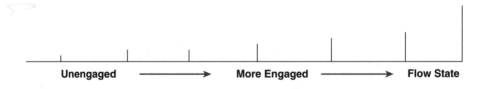

If we have flow as our teaching goal, any approximation to it (i.e., any point along the continuum beyond unengaged) will further learning. Good teachers want engaged students. They also want students to progress in academic achievement. But engagement and achievement are not two sides of that familiar coin. In the best moments of classroom life, students are engaged and achieving at the same time. Thoughtful teachers search for teaching practices and classroom conditions that will initiate and sustain engagement while also effecting achievement and accomplishment.

Chapter 2, "Engaged Brains," presents the research on brain-based learning, which has intensified in the last two decades. Teaching practices engage learners *naturally* when practice is grounded in neurological research on the human brain, for what is more natural than aligning teaching practices with how brains learn in any setting? By *neurological* I mean brain-based principles and insights derived from brain science. When I speak of *brain* or *mind*, I mean that mass of tissue between our ears and the electrochemical activity that goes on there. I use the terms interchangeably, agreeing with brain researchers Berninger and Richards (2002) that "the mind is the brain at work" (p. 3). It's not my purpose here, nor my desire, to enter into the important discussions on the origins of mind or the distinctions between mind and brain as some philosophers might.

Chapter 3, "Engaged Hearts," discusses elements of spiritual engagement that derive from humanistic theory. By *humanistic* I mean those principles that derive from experiences in our lives that we say are "from the heart" or that some would call "spiritual." I use the word *heart* as the conceptual counterpart to *spirit*. Both words refer to that which is more than neurological and which involves subjectivity, higher-order thinking, and connections with something larger than the self. Although many people hold that spiritual events are really just physiological, I believe that keeping matters of the heart distinct from matters of the brain is more useful for understanding the nature of engaged learning. To say that one is spiritually engaged is different from saying that one is cognitively engaged. My use of the terms *heart* and *spirit* represent a humanistic perspective.

I emphasize mindfulness, compassion, and unity as the humanistic experiences common to most people. For stylistic variation, I often use the terms *humanistic, heart-based*, and *spiritual* interchangeably. When the brain and the heart are engaged in learning, people experience flow states. Such learning states are the ultimate experiential goal for our students and the immediate practical goal for us as their teachers.

Genuine engagement affects both brains and hearts, not one or the other. We lose powerful insights from science and from humanistic theory when we think in either-or terms—if we think we *either* have brain-compatible approaches *or* we have heart-based approaches. Parker Palmer (1998) warns of the dangers of such either-or thinking:

> Many of us live one-eyed lives. We rely largely on the eye of the mind to form our image of reality. But today more and more of us are opening the other eye, the eye of the heart, looking for realities to which the mind's eye is blind. Either eye alone is not enough. We need "Wholesight," a vision of the world in which mind and heart unite "as my two eyes make one in sight." (p. xxiii)

Teaching and learning, Palmer (1998/1999) says, "require us to think 'both-and' instead of 'either-or.' That is Wholesight. Teaching and learning are done not by disembodied intellects but by whole persons whose brains cannot be disconnected from feeling and spirit, from heart and soul" (p. 10). An eye turned toward a world of fact and reason, one that ignores the world of feeling and spirit, is dangerous. It is equally dangerous to become one-eyed in the other direction by ignoring the empirical world. Palmer would have us embrace both worlds.

Although I discuss brain-based learning and heart-based learning separately, it is only a temporary separation. Chapter 4, "Engagement and Instructional Practice," synthesizes brain-based research and heart-based elements into a framework for teaching practices. In this chapter, I present groups of questions that connect research with theory and practice. These questions are intended to guide teachers in making decisions about teaching practices based on a deep understanding of student minds and hearts when they're truly engaged in learning.

Engagement as Flow

Think of truly engaged learning as being in a *flow state.* Flow is what people of all ages describe when they become totally immersed in something—a hobby, such as woodworking; a talent, such as playing the flute; a sport; a problem, such as resolving a dispute; or a wondering, such as wondering how stem cell research works. Here, for example, is how one person describes engagement in the experience of art:

> When I see works that come close to my heart, that I think are really fine, I have the strangest reaction: which is not always exhilarating, it is sort of like being hit in the stomach. Feeling a little nauseous. It's just this sort of completely overwhelming feeling, which then I have to grope my way out of, calm myself down, and try to approach it scientifically. . . . What comes to you after looking at it calmly, after you've really digested every nuance and every little thread, is the total impact. When you encounter a great work of art, you just know it and it thrills you in all your senses, not just visually, but sensually and intellectually. (Csikszentmihalyi, 1990a, p. 107)

If understanding the conditions that create flow states can help us understand better the nature of engagement in *any* activity, then we can find ways of nurturing engagement in the specific learning events of classrooms, elementary to university, in any subject. Engaged learning goes beyond superficial knowledge, such as memorizing facts or filling in forms, to more complex, more compelling meaning.

ENGAGEMENT

Each of us can recall a time in our lives when we felt intense focus. We may have cozied up on a dreary winter day to read a compelling mystery—getting lost in an imaginary world of twists, clues, and tensions. Or we may have leaned over the fender of a car and listened intently to the engine, our ears picking up the nuances of engine sounds. We may have sat in the kitchen with Aunt Mary, canning peaches, busily peeling fruit and reminiscing about days long past, relatives long gone—the afternoon slipping away in easy conversation. Perhaps we were involved in intense competition—the final passionate seconds of a volleyball tournament, the last inning in a close softball game, or the final half mile of a marathon. Maybe we were enjoying a hobby or a talent, such as the time we happened upon a 1952D dime to add to our coin collection, the day we found ourselves talking to our backyard plot of rhododendrons while fertilizing them, or the evening we sat at the piano and played *Für Elise* straight through for the first time.

Engaging moments, all. But what do events such as these teach us about the nature of engagement? When we reflect on them, what can we tease out that would illuminate engaged moments like these?

For one, each time of engagement involved some type of *energy*. This is the energy expressed in the verbs section of the definition of *engagement* from the *Oxford English Dictionary* (OED) (1989): "to cause to be held fast; to involve, to entangle." Notice the sense of volition in the extended OED definition: "to fasten, attach . . . to interlock with . . . to entangle, involve, commit, mix up . . . to attract and hold fast (attention, interest) . . . to enter up or employ oneself in an action."

Second, such events show us that engagement can be cognitive, emotional, or physical, as some research has indicated (Fredericks, Blumenfeld, & Paris, 2004). Thus, running a race can be just as engaging as writing a story, reading a book, or solving a math problem. Moments of engagement may take place alone or with others: For some of us, solitude may be just the right condition for becoming engaged, while others may need to have people around.

Engagement may also be spiritual when it seems to transcend time and space (e.g., lost in a book) or when it helps us identify with something beyond ourselves (e.g., empathy for a character in a film). While canning peaches with Aunt Mary, time seems to slip by unawares; while reading a magazine in the grocery line, we fail to notice that the line has advanced but we have not; while taking in a compelling work of art, we lose ourselves in the aesthetic moment. In these moments of transcendence, we may also become connected with timeless qualities such as love, compassion, and wonder, as Scott Russell Sanders (1999) describes when he writes about those moments when he experiences beauty. In the following passage, Ruth is his daughter.

> Now and again some voice raised on the stairs leading to my study, some passage of music, some noise on the street, will stir a sympathetic thrum from the strings of the guitar that tilts against the wall just behind my door. Just so, over and over again, impulses from the world stir a responsive chord in me—not just any chord, but a particular one, combining notes of elegance, exhilaration, simplicity, and awe. The feeling is as recognizable to me, as unmistakable, as the sound of Ruth's voice or the beating of my own heart. A screech owl calls, a comet streaks the night sky, a story moves unerringly to a close, a child lays an arrowhead in the palm of my hand, my daughter smiles at me through her bridal veil, and I feel for a moment at peace, in place, content. I sense in those momentary encounters a harmony, between myself and whatever I behold. The word that seems to fit most exactly this feeling of resonance, this sympathetic vibration between inside and outside, is beauty. (p. 246)

ENGAGEMENT AS FLOW

As Sanders' encounter with beauty illustrates, engagement is often intimately connected with our happiness. In the moment of engagement, he experiences a state of bliss, a "sympathetic vibration between inside and outside." Another, more familiar, term describing this state is *flow*, as used principally by Csikszentmihalyi and his associates (Csikszentmihalyi, Rathunde, Whalen, & Wong, 1993), who have studied the optimal experiences of complete engagement: "Flow is a subjective state that people report when they are completely involved in something to the point of losing track of time and of being unaware of fatigue and of everything else but the activity itself" (p. 14). Mary Rose O'Reilley (2000)—writer, teacher, and spiritual seeker—describes her experience of flow when engaged as a member of a singing group:

> Singing this music is something like what I think psychologists call "abreaction"—when they flood the system with psychoactive drugs

or stab a probe into a lizard brain or do whatever they do to cause a complete reorganization and downloading of the mental systems. The singing over, we drop like birds who have been buffeted to the edge of the oxygen zone. We have barely escaped with our lives. (p. 51)

Csikszentmihalyi's research (1990a) shows the range of such experiences, as in these examples:

A dancer describes how it feels when a performance is going well: "Your concentration is very complete. Your mind isn't wandering, you are not thinking of something else; you are totally involved in what you are doing. . . . Your energy is flowing very smoothly. You feel relaxed, comfortable, and energetic."

A mother who enjoys time spent with her small daughter: "Her reading is the one thing that she's really into, and we read together. She reads to me, and I read to her, and that's a time when I sort of lose touch with the rest of the world, I'm totally absorbed in what I'm doing." (p. 53)

Our flow experiences can come from work or play, during times of tension or relaxation, with great complexity or simplicity, by oneself or with others.

It could be singing in a choir, programming a computer, dancing, playing bridge, reading a good book. Or if you love your job, as many people do, it could be when you are getting immersed in a complicated surgical procedure or a close business deal. Or this complete immersion in the activity may occur in a social interaction, as when friends talk with each other, or when a mother plays with her baby. (Csikszentmihalyi, 1997, p. 29)

Flow is present enough in most of our lives, to some degree, that we know what it is like to be completely and fully engaged. It generally brings pleasure, as in singing or reading, but not always, such as in a heated argument with a partner or spouse, or in an intense jury deliberation. Flow in school, however, needs to be intellectually or emotionally pleasurable if it is to be successful as a learning experience: The most engaging learning involves sufficient challenge at just the right level of skill, as explained below.

If flow is the ultimate state of engagement, and if flow experiences can occur in any kind of human activity, why shouldn't we make it our goal for teaching? That is to say, if we understand the nature of total engagement, why would we not align our teaching practices with the conditions that create flow? You might be thinking that flow occurs infrequently, under only the most ideal conditions, when the learner is deeply and personally committed to the flow activity. You might say that it is impossible to create flow in classrooms all the time. Probably so, but that is also the very reason why we should work to create flow. Any genuine approximation to a flow state is tantamount to engaged learning—at some level, to some degree. It is an ideal goal, certainly, but also a realistic one that is rooted in the most fundamental of our common experiences as learners: our personal encounters with flow. Indeed, most, if not all of us, went into teaching because we were passionate about our own learning experiences—either with our subject matter or working with young people or both. Upon reflection, we might recall a number of peak experiences that made us want to foster more of the same as a teacher. A high school science teacher told me, "I went into science because I was passionate about how things work, driven to understand the natural world, and I want my students to share that passion." A middle school language arts teacher selected English as her major because she "just loved reading and being around language"; she said that she teaches "because in my heart and soul I want my students to love reading too!" An elementary teacher reported that "As a kid and then as a young adult, I always had this weird curiosity about things—books, bugs, magic, just about everything—and I wanted to bring out that same curiosity in children; I wanted them to savor that part of themselves where curiosity lives, before other things in the world try to knock it out of them."

Flow and engaged learning go hand in hand, as Csikszentmihalyi (1997) points out: "The flow experience acts as a magnet for learning—that is, for developing new levels of challenges and skills" (p. 33). Engagement defined as flow gives us a goal that our own personal experiences have shown is reachable. How to inculcate such genuinely engaged learning is not a simple matter of incorporating the latest pedagogy, finding *the* proven method, implementing new software, or moving classroom furniture. We must first understand what it means when our brains and our hearts enter into flow states of engagement.

THE CONDITIONS OF FLOW

According to Csikszentmihalyi and his colleagues (1993, p. 14), flow states exhibit five common conditions, and teachers can strongly influence the first three conditions. People experiencing flow

- have *clear goals*. They know what they want and they know the procedures to follow to get it. For example, they follow the musical score in order to complete the piece on the piano, or they listen well and respond thoughtfully if they wish the dinner conversation with friends to continue to be engaging. Likewise, we can help students understand the goals for classroom activities in which *they* engage. For example, we can help them know their purpose for reading, say, an expository essay, so that they can judge what is relevant, and what is not, to their purpose in reading it (Tovani, 2005). Similarly, in a math class, we can help students understand that the purpose of a particular math procedure is not to find the correct answer but to find more than one way of solving the problem.

- get *feedback* on their performance that is immediate and relevant to their performance. For instance, when they strike the wrong piano keys or play the wrong chord, their ears provide the feedback needed in order to make adjustments. When they devalue their friends' views, they put up conversation stoppers. In school, we can easily set up feedback loops. For example, having students write in a reading journal *while* reading helps them self-monitor their developing understanding of an essay; likewise, using a study buddy to check their tentative answer to a math problem can provide students with immediate feedback.

- find that the level of challenge and ability to meet the challenge are in *balance*. When challenge exceeds skill, people feel defeated. When skill exceeds challenge, they get bored. Beginning pianists wouldn't attempt a Mozart concerto, nor would people comfortably enter into conversation when they know little about the topic at hand or have little interest in it. We provide balance when we differentiate instruction for diverse learners. We also plan for balance when we use assessments (e.g., reading, writing, math, concept understanding) to gauge students' skill levels in order to apportion tasks to match those skill levels.

With the next two conditions—concentration and enjoyment—we have some influence but much less control because concentration and enjoyment come from within oneself. In flow states, people

- *concentrate*, to the point of temporarily forgetting worries or losing track of time. At the piano, again, they forget to make a needed phone call or turn off the oven because they are lost in the music; at the dinner table, they suddenly realize that the engrossing after-dinner talk has made hours pass like minutes. In a classroom, we can structure the environment to help students concentrate—for example, through creating quiet corners, offering uninterrupted reading or writing, or by playing quiet background music. Some teachers even have noise-canceling headphones or firefighters' ear-muffs handy for students to use if desired.

- *enjoy* the activity for its own sake (even when it is difficult or dangerous). They linger at the piano even when they are tired of practicing. They invite friends back for dinner because they so enjoy their company. In classrooms, teachers who visibly enjoy the subjects they teach have a greater chance of bringing that joy to their students. Teachers can celebrate what they enjoy about their subjects. For example, teachers who enjoy writing can present writing as an enjoyable activity; history teachers who enjoy reading can easily share with students their reading pleasures. I know math teachers for whom the symmetry of math is a source of great pleasure; in their classrooms, I witness regular explosions of joy when their students solve math problems. We may not be able to *make* students enjoy their subjects, but we can go a long way toward encouraging enjoyment.

Flow can and does occur in school, though not nearly as much as it could. That it more likely takes place outside of school was discovered by Smith and Wilhelm (2002) when they compared adolescent boys' reading lives in and out of school: "What we found in our study is that all of the young men with whom we worked were passionate about some activity. They experienced flow. But, unfortunately, most of them did not experience it in their literate activity, at least not in school" (p. 30). These researchers recommend that, when planning instruction, we focus on the quality of students' daily experiences in the classroom by working "to create the conditions that will make students more inclined to engage in learning what they need to know. These conditions are those of 'flow' experiences" (p. 53).

As these researchers suggest, aiming for flow states is a realistic goal if we wish to approximate, in classrooms, the passion that students report experiencing outside school. Working successfully toward such states by teaching to the brains and hearts of learners is more likely to put student learning on the spectrum of engagement leading toward flow states.

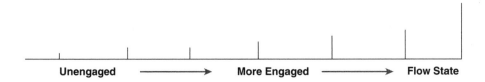

Unengaged ⟶ **More Engaged** ⟶ **Flow State**

Because learners can be more—or less—engaged, they need not be in a pure flow state in order to experience some level of engagement: Any approximation to flow is therefore engaging. As we know more about how *brains* and *hearts* become engaged in learning, we are more able to base instructional practice on these two foundations.

Engaged Brains

Teachers and school communities today find themselves pressured to conduct their work through a view of research that is not very helpful for understanding engagement. It is a narrow vision, and it is supported by powerful political and economic forces (e.g., test results–driven political campaigns, software and textbook companies). No Child Left Behind (NCLB) legislation, for example, has put a premium on "scientifically based" reading approaches that currently enjoy political popularity. Some (e.g., Kozol, 2005) believe that the NCLB version of science atomizes curricula, revitalizes behavioral psychology, and counts as valuable only that which can be counted.

Another view of scientifically based research exists that is more helpful for understanding engagement: brain science. In recent years, insights into how learning brains work have yielded rich findings and have suggested many implications for understanding engaged learning. Neurobiologists have been cautious about making specific claims about what neurological research means for particular classroom practice. "Science generates knowledge and conceptual frameworks that teachers can draw upon in planning their instructional programs, but science does not specify exactly how to implement that knowledge on a daily basis," write Berninger and Richards (2002). It should be teachers, they recommend, "who evaluate the best way to implement that new knowledge in their classrooms" (p. 313).

Brain-based learning, then, is not a set of practices; it is a set of understandings about how brains work based on neuroscientific research. These understandings can help us plan instruction aimed at increasing engagement. Storytelling, for example, when seen as brain-based practice, takes on increased significance in the classroom. We all know that students might pay more attention when we tell stories, so there's nothing new in that understanding. But, from a brain-based view, storytelling actually helps some brains learn better by appealing to multiple memory pathways. When my psychology friend (see Preface) told his story about the high school reunion as a way to illustrate standard error of measurement, he drew on multiple memory pathways in his students' brains to gain their attention. He used *semantic pathways* by telling the story in words. Because there was some conflict between people in the vignette, students' *emotional memory pathways* were involved. And because the story took place in a particular setting (Ohio) and time (a weekend), it appealed to students' *episodic memory pathways.* Given the way good stories engage learners, it is no surprise that we remember the stories teachers tell far more than we remember the content of their expository talk.

Neuroscientific research about the brain challenges, supports, and enriches teaching practices. If we wish to claim a scientific foundation for understanding engagement, we must keep our attention tuned to principles based on neurological findings, and they are numerous (Caine & Caine, 1994, 1997; Jensen, 1998; Lyons, 2003; Sylwester, 1995, 2003; Wolfe & Brandt, 1998). Combined, these principles coalesce around three essential findings.

#1: BRAINS SEARCH FOR MEANING

Nerve synapses—"neural forests"—constitute the wiring diagram of the brain. Learning occurs when brains make synaptic connections, and brain cells connect when there is a reason to do so. Neurons connect when the brain finds something meaningful or desires to make something meaningful. If it is not meaning*ful,* then it must be meaning*less.* You can't have it both ways. What is meaning*less* is quickly neurologically pruned. If learners are not making meaning or not searching to make meaning, they are not, by definition, truly learning. That is a scientific fact. To know just how true this is, we need only recall cramming facts into our brains the night before an exam, only to scarcely remember them again once the exam ended. Or we need only recall listening to a lecture that was "way over our heads" to know that what doesn't connect with what we already know is not learned.

Meaningfulness, then, is the purpose for learning as well as for teaching, as Brooks (2004) states emphatically: "Searching for meaning is the purpose of learning, so teaching for meaning is the purpose of teaching. If we do not have meaning making at the core of our pedagogy and practice, then let's not call the activity *teaching*. Doing so demeans the word and the noble art and science it represents" (p. 9). The meaning-making activity of the brain has to be coherent if it is to make sense, as neurophilosopher Patricia Smith Churchland (2004) points out: "Indeed, we know that brains are continually organizing, structuring, extracting, and creating. As a central part of their predictive functions, nervous systems are rigged to make a coherent story of whatever input they get. 'Coherencing,' as I call it" (p. 50).

From the perspective of the human brain, if we really want to make learning meaningful, there are a number of ways we can engage students' brains.

Looking for Meaningful Patterns

When Mrs. Murphy begins her unit on the American Civil War, she places a large cardboard box in the middle of her classroom. The box contains copies of various printed materials from the 1850s to 1862—newspaper articles and editorials, broadsheets, poems, songs, and personal letters. She asks her juniors to pair up and read as much of the materials as they can in two to three days, while looking for patterns that suggest why this country was in a prewar state. From their reading, they are to develop a theory on the causes of the war.

The human brain seeks out patterns in information because patterns present data that connect somehow, as Mrs. Murphy's students are likely to discover for themselves. Likewise, when students notice the artistry in a poem, they observe the ways certain things seem to go together—such as how words reflect the sounds of other words to form rhyme patterns or how images relate to one another. When math students closely examine large sets of mathematical data, nothing makes sense until their brains perceive patterns in the data. In Mrs. Murphy's American history class, over the course of the year, students come to understand the continuity of human history by recognizing that seemingly disparate historical events have common patterns, such as the collusion of power and greed or the engendering of fear and/or nationalism, when countries mobilize for war.

Constructing Personal Theories

For many teachers, "teaching" means telling students about something—in didactic ways. But in Mr. Enriquez's English class, students preparing to read Dr. Martin Luther King's "Letter From a Birmingham Jail" are not told in advance why Dr. King forgives his enemies. Instead, Mr. Enriquez asks them to read King's famous letter and discern for themselves his motivations. Their act of discerning constitutes the construction of their personal theory—saying, in effect, "Based on what I've read, here is what I think motivated Dr. King." They will have to read closely and critically: sorting through the data, tentatively forming hypotheses, perhaps comparing their emerging theories with peers, and then possibly revising their hypotheses.

When we grapple with problems on our own or in the company of others, when we spend time closely observing a natural phenomenon (e.g., a leaf), and when we notice the way a character develops throughout the course of a novel, we construct our understanding of the problem, the leaf, or the character. Looking for patterns in the information and connecting them with prior knowledge or a known purpose, we piece together, bit by bit, our personal meaning. This, again, is a *natural* way the brain learns—by building a personal theory based upon synaptic connections, held tentatively until confirmed. Our personal meanings become our understanding, and they become more valid as we find more connections that confirm or modify our theory. This hypothesis building is how many of us learned to play a sport before ever being formally coached. It is how we learned to trust or distrust others based on our history of personal interactions with them. And it is how we learned to navigate the Internet without having formal instruction. In each instance, we constructed mental models ourselves, and as time went on, we elaborated upon or revised those models. Constructivism is eminently brain based, as has been shown repeatedly in brain research (for a good summary, see Brooks, 2004; for a good introduction to constructivist teaching and a solid rationale, see Brooks & Brooks, 1999).

We can engage the brains of students through constructivist pedagogy in many ways, for the process is simple *theory building:* Provide students with a lot of information and a purpose for analyzing it; allow them to sort through that information, looking for connections; have them articulate (through talking, writing, or drawing) their tentative theory; and then let them try out their theory (e.g., by comparing it with the constructed theories of other students). In language arts, for example, we can teach genres of writing such as memoir through constructivism by exposing students to many examples of memoir and inviting them to create their own theory of memoir as genre. Through such integrated reading and writing, students develop procedural knowledge—how to write memoir—that derives from reading for a purpose—to determine what *is* memoir. As another example, this time in mathematics, students' predictions become their tentatively constructed theory when they are given this experiment in calculating wasted water: "In this experiment you will simulate a leaking faucet and collect data about the volume of water lost at 5-second intervals. You will then use the patterns in your results to predict how much water is wasted when a faucet leaks for one month" (Lappan, Fey, Fitzgerald, Friel, & Phillips, 2004, p. 6).

Paying Attention in Personally Significant Ways

Mr. Cook, a middle school teacher, prepares a social studies unit on democracy in ancient Greece. He plans to introduce the unit by explaining to students the major tenets of democracy and illustrating them by comparing ancient Greece with the United States today. "That will make it relevant to them," he says, "because they live in a democratic country."

Maybe. But if he thinks in terms of student brains, the concept *democracy* will be more relevant if he can help them understand how democracy (or the lack thereof) is present in their daily lives. "How," he might ask his students, "do you decide, with friends, what DVD to rent? Or how are major decisions made in your families—by a parent only or through negotiation and agreement among other family members?" With Mr. Cook's students, democracy is relevant because they have had previous direct experiences with democratic structures and environments, though they may not have called it that. They already know what democracy is; they just don't know it in this new way. Once they know democracy personally, they will more easily come to know democracy in more distant, less personal ways.

You pay attention to something for a number of reasons. If it is relevant to what you already know, as in the democracy example, then you pay more attention to it. You activate prior knowledge. You also pay attention if you have to make decisions or value judgments, such as choosing what is more or less important to a particular goal, what is easier or harder, better or worse, and so on. If, for instance, language arts students are tasked with deciding the three most important clues in, say, a Poe short story, then out of all the possible clues they discover, what seems less important will not capture their brain's attention; the brain will consider some things relevant to what's important and other things not relevant to what's important.

You also pay attention when you try to find a sense of order in what at first seems chaotic. Attention is an active search for information that brings pleasure once that information becomes meaningful. Hence, the flow experience when we finally shout, "Eureka!" as Archimedes is reputed to have done in discovering the law of buoyancy. When confronted with contradiction or paradox, brains seek to resolve the *cognitive dissonance*—if they care about it. Brains want to resolve contradiction; they prefer order to chaos, certainty over doubt. A history teacher asked students how it could be that Saddam Hussein could be considered both good and evil. While it was easy for them to come up with the many ways he is considered evil, students struggled to find ways in which they could consider him good. This teacher's wise challenge built upon her knowledge of how brains want to resolve tension. Once the brain senses that resolution is imminent, a state of pleasure is just on the horizon: "'Getting it' really is thrilling. The sheer pleasure and joy of insight is so great that it is intrinsically motivating and keeps people going," say Caine and Caine (2001, p. 46).

You also attend to what matters to you *emotionally.* While I discuss emotions and the brain in detail below, it is worth noting briefly here that when we encounter learning that hearkens to emotional memories, we pay closer attention. When Ms. Sands, a sixth-grade teacher, introduced a story with betrayal as its central theme, she had students write in their reading journals about a time when someone betrayed them or they betrayed someone else. Once they recalled betrayal from their emotional memories, they were ready to read attentively about someone else's experience with betrayal.

#2: EMOTIONS DRIVE BRAINS IN LEARNING

Emotions have biological pathways in the brain. Isn't it ironic, therefore, when emotional components of learning are so ignored, as Sylwester (1995) points out:

> Our profession pays lip service to educating the whole student, but school activities tend to focus on the development of measurable, rational qualities. We measure students' spelling accuracy, not their emotional well being. And when the budget gets tight, we cut the difficult-to-measure curricular areas, such as the arts, that tilt toward emotion. We know emotion is very important to the educative process because it drives attention, which drives learning and memory. (p. 72)

Many researchers have presented substantive evidence for the emotional underpinnings of learning. LeDoux (1996), for example, argues that "brain states and bodily responses are the fundamental facts of an emotion" (p. 302). According to Pert (1997), molecules of emotion travel throughout our body and brain to influence the thinking and behavior involved in learning.

Emotions are intimately connected with students' beliefs about themselves as learners. Positive beliefs allow them to take on new challenges with gusto. Discussing motivation for learning, Jensen (1998) describes two types of confidence that influence learners' attitudes toward success—"The learner's content beliefs ('I have the ability to learn this subject') and context beliefs ('I have the interest and resources to succeed in *this class* with *this teacher*')." Jensen notes that these beliefs "create states that release powerful brain chemicals. Positive thinking . . . triggers the release of pleasure chemicals like dopamine as well as natural opiates, or endorphins. This self-reward reinforces the desired behavior" (p. 64).

Negative beliefs help students learn how to be helpless. When they exhibit "learned helplessness," they communicate to us (in subtle and not-so-subtle ways) that they "are no good" at a subject or that they are likely to be unsuccessful. The brain knows threat when it feels it. The neurological result of such threat is called *downshifting,* "a psychophysiological response to perceived threat accompanied by a sense of helplessness and lack of self-efficacy. . . . When we downshift, we revert to the tried and true—and follow old beliefs and behaviors regardless of what information the road signs provide" (Caine & Caine, 1994, pp. 69–70). For instance, when students are forced to read texts that are beyond their reach, they often downshift by avoiding the reading, "forgetting" to do the reading, blaming themselves for being poor readers, or becoming behavior problems to draw attention away from their challenges.

Reversing these emotional states is possible—with many, many positive experiences that "counteraffect" negative emotional memories, as Jensen (1998) points out: "Students who have learned to be helpless may need dozens of positive choice trials before becoming mobilized again. The brain must rewire itself to change the behavior" (p. 58). Mark Twain was onto this when he pointed out that a cat that sits on a hot stove will never sit on a hot stove again—or a cold one!

Social-emotional interactions contribute to engagement. Witness the popularity, among students, of group projects, peer writing groups, literature circles, and other forms of collaborative work. Interactions like these sustain curiosity and wonder, promote experimentation with and refinement of ideas, challenge and support learning, enhance abilities to solve problems collaboratively, build relationships of trust and respect for difference, and further individual growth in "emotional intelligence" (Goleman, 1995). While many people can reach flow states when they are alone, such as when they are reading and writing, playing music, and working out, many, if not most, students thrive in the midst of other learners (Vygotsky, 1978). "The brain is a social brain," write Caine and Caine (1997, p. 104), and social interactions charge emotions.

#3: ENGAGED BRAINS
ENGENDER MIND-BODY STATES

In middle school and high school, Ben never did well in science. And yet, when he was in elementary school, he loved science—especially the parts that piqued his curiosity and made him feel like a scientist. Something changed when he got to middle school, however, and it continued on into high school. When asked about the difference, he said,

> In elementary school we used to put on old sneakers and shorts and walk down streams looking for bugs and fish, and in the classroom we would make "machines" out of junk that we really thought would solve big problems like pollution. We would have science notebooks and go around the school noticing how different plants lived in different areas—what grew better where and that kind of stuff. Sometimes I just got completely lost in a science project, and teachers would have to bring me back to reality. But then in middle school, science was all about textbooks and lists of names and Friday quizzes. We never walked down Cherry Creek again. That was when I started hating science.

When Ben "got completely lost in a science project," he experienced *mind-body states of flow,* powerful holistic conditions chemically induced in engaged moments. These are the chemicals that, when activated naturally or introduced into the body as medication, affect us emotionally, intellectually, and bodily. They travel throughout the body and influence everything from what we think we can or cannot do to what we are willing or not willing to do. They create interconnections between what we think and how we feel (emotionally and physically) that ultimately dictate attention and behavior at any given moment.

Sylwester (2003) calls this interconnectivity the "bodybrain" (p. 18), while Pert (1997) refers to it as "bodymind" (p. 187). The most optimal mind-body state would be when the brain is most comfortable: We do not sense threat but rather safety; stress may be present but not to the extent that it causes threat. We get a feeling of "relaxed alertness," a state marked by low threat and high challenge and considered by brain researchers to be the "optimal state of mind for meaningful learning" (Caine & Caine, 1994, p. 140). Stress is not equivalent to threat: "For teachers, it is a matter of taking students beyond their comfort zone without undue threat" (Caine & Caine, 1994, p. 141). Caine and Caine (1994) explain that

Relaxed alertedness . . . is a dynamic state that is compatible with a great deal of change. . . . There is the curiosity we have when we want to find out why something works. There is a sense of expectancy that we have while anticipating the outcome or possible development of an issue or situation. There is the overwhelming sense of awe that often accompanies great art, music and scientific discovery. There is even some fear of the unknown. (pp. 143–144)

Envisioning learning as mind-body states changes the ways we think about practice. For instance, in order to bring about more engaged learning through *cognitive dissonance,* we would plan lessons marked by deliberate tensions, such as presenting paradoxes and challenges to normal ways of thinking: presenting two conflicting sets of data in math or science or suggesting alternative interpretations of a text. If we wish to encourage states of *relaxed alertness,* we would practice the sort of "playfulness" advocated by Caine and Caine (1994), whereby we model "a willingness to experiment, an openness to unexpected consequences, and a sense of positive anticipation or expectancy"—for playfulness "can do a great deal to help students lose fear; break through to new knowledge; and go beyond what they, and their teacher, believe to be their capacity to learn. The key is to build the play around the content" (p. 146).

If we consider teaching practices in light of these three major findings, we would approach our work with students more thoughtfully, with more respect for brains and how they work. "What will I do on Monday?" to borrow an old saw, would become "How will I engage my students' brains on Monday to learn the content of the curriculum and to develop skills?" While this way of thinking will move us toward practices that engage students' brains, we must add to that ways of thinking that engage their hearts as well.

Engaged Hearts

Every so often, I have this conversation with a biologist friend. We're talking about teaching and I say something about engaging students' brains *and* hearts. He laughs and says that everything we need to know about engaged learning is neurological. "Engaged hearts," he says, "are nothing more than neurons in the brain. Francis Crick called it the 'astonishing hypothesis,' whereby all thinking and feeling occur physiologically in the brain."

"But," I say, "heart is just a metaphor for something that is more than neurological." And before he can say, "No such thing," I rattle on about how people are more than the sum of their molecular parts, how purely mechanistic views of people easily lead to a narrow reductionism, and how, until the day science can explain what are called "matters of the heart," he and I will continue to have this conversation, as so many others have before us, and so many others will after us.

It is a philosophical issue, one that philosophers, scientists, and neurophilosophers often debate. Brain research being still in its infancy, it is too soon to accept a mechanistic view of self. That being the case, let us then examine engagement from an alternate but complementary perspective—one that may well turn out to be purely neurological one day but that, for now, still registers with us as certain experiences that we may call humanistic and heart-based, and that still has as much promise for driving learning as do neurons.

I use the word *spirit* interchangeably with *heart*. I consider *spiritual* here in the secular, not the religious, sense, and I mean it to include emotional lives as well as other traditional humanitarian experiences such as *compassion* and *connectedness*, as explained below. Talking about spiritual matters in teaching creates discomfort for many people, and I think I know why: Spirituality challenges the world of empiricism that education so values and suggests to many people forces and experiences that cannot be measured, aren't "real," and therefore aren't very important. Yet, as Parker Palmer says, "What is inward and invisible is at least as important as what is outward and empirical" (as quoted in O'Reilley, 1998, p. x). James Moffett (1994) considered avoiding "the word spirituality because it makes red flags pop up in many minds—unctuous sermons by preachers . . . millionaire TV evangelists preying on the frail, superstition blocking the progress of science, religion as the opiate of the masses" (p. 17). Red flags popping up aside, I believe most of us know some kind of spiritual, heart-based engagement firsthand. We ought not, then, eschew humanitarian matters—or spirit—from teaching, where, as I will also show, it is intimately bound up with engaged learning.

In shying away from the humanitarian, we devalue those dimensions of engagement that touch the human heart. Notice, for example, how these people speak of their flow experiences as expansive human moments:

- A dancer reports, "A strong relaxation and calmness comes over me. I have no worries of failure. What a powerful and warm feeling it is! I want to expand to hug the world. I feel enormous power to effect something of grace and beauty."
- A climber says, "It's a Zen feeling, like meditation or concentration. One thing you're after is the one-pointedness of mind." (Csikszentmihalyi 1990a, pp. 59–60)

We are creatures of both brains *and* hearts, and when *both* are engaged, compelling learning erupts. We need to ground our ways of thinking about engaged hearts in our own personal histories, in our felt sense of spiritual engagement. Charles Suhor (1998/1999), writing about engaged hearts in classrooms, would have us reflect on "the central and defining experiences of our lives," those times when we have experienced something much more than cognitive:

- *Aesthetic experience:* "Most adults have been powerfully elevated by some art form, whether as artist-maker or recipient-perceiver."
- *Person-to-person contact:* "The most accessible spiritual experiences are deep love for, and close communication with, other people."

- *Inner experience:* Suhor cites the stockbroker who sees relationships in market data, or a mathematician who notices a symmetry that generates a new formula, "or a writer—you or I—discovering the most apt phrasing for an idea. . . . Many of us can report inner experiences in which we have glimpsed a thrilling truth and had a sudden, refreshing sense of spaciousness."
- *Communing with nature:* "People often speak with deep conviction about moments of communion with nature."
- *Sensory experience:* "The 'high' experienced by athletes brings an unmistakably spiritual release." So do t'ai chi, aikido, fencing, and childbirth, as examples.
- *Extrasensory experience:* Such experiences as clairvoyance, distance healing, out-of-body experiences, and telekinesis can provide a felt sense of deep engagement.
- *Ceremony and ritual:* Think of the jazz funeral or the old-order Catholic High Mass in Latin, both of which may connect the individual with something larger than the self—death and life in the funeral, and the divine in the Mass. (pp. 14–15)

Experiences like these, writes Suhor (1998/1999), give a person an opportunity to form a beyond-ego relationship that connects self with a deeper self—as in meditation—or with other—for example, an idea or cause, nature, religion, art, or people.

Upon closer examination of Suhor's (1998/1999) categories, we find that three elements, or themes, emerge:

- Mindfulness
- Unity
- Compassion

These three themes constitute a foundation for engaged learning from a spiritual perspective, for these themes cut across much rich humanistic theory and many teaching practices that enable the hearts of learners. I examine these themes in more detail for the insight they provide in furthering our understanding of engagement as flow.

#1: MINDFULNESS

When Mr. Martin teaches writing, he wants students to use specific details. He tells them to "show, not tell," by which he means for them to use concrete images (not "Crackerjacks are really good" but "Crackerjacks melt on your tongue, stick to your teeth, and fill the hidden crannies in your rear gum line, but it's mainly the caramel that keeps you grabbing handful after handful"). He urges students to name products (not "junk food breakfast" but "Toaster Pops"). And he coaches them to rely on the sensory facts of verisimilitude (not "My uncle acted weird," but "My uncle never wore two socks that matched"). When, for example, he has his writers describe meals in the cafeteria, he tasks them with many hands-on "showing exercises" (for a discussion of showing exercises, see Caplan & Keech, 1990) and then sends them to the cafeteria with their writer's notebooks and has them write down all the observations they can make while other students have lunch. He encourages them to become *mindful* writers.

Becoming mindful means that a person pays close attention to everything, internal and external, as Mary Rose O'Reilley (1998), teacher and practitioner of mindfulness, says about what builds the contemplative life: "Mindfulness [is the] practice of simply being there, with a very precise and focused attention, listening, watching. Not being somewhere else, answering some question that hasn't been asked" (p. 3).

It is mindfulness that botanists rely on when they observe plant growth. It is mindfulness that jazz musicians must have if they are to become attuned to the others in a jazz ensemble. Writers are doomed to failure without it: "The . . . writing life—depends above all on fidelity to objects," writes O'Reilley (2000, p. 95). Teachers practice mindfulness when they make special efforts to value each student in their charge—for instance, when they notice what students are wearing, what they say in class, their hobbies and interests, their *lives*. And they practice mindfulness when they truly listen to students, as O'Reilley (1998) says, "with absolute taking-in of the other" (p. 31).

We see mindfulness in democratic classrooms, where teachers and students habitually learn from one another because they notice the teacher and the learner in one another; in science labs where students grow plants, tracking and measuring weekly changes; in social studies classrooms where students imaginatively enter into the lives of historical figures or the cultures of bygone eras; and in literature discussions where character analysis comes about by noticing closely what a character *says* and *does*. In each case, students must attend to the particulars, not the generalities—up close rather than distant.

#2: UNITY

When Ms. Lee teaches young people about the early days of the American Civil Rights Movement, she tries to connect the big story of American history with the little stories of their personal histories. She knows that because the students were not alive at that time, there's a good chance that this crucial historical period will be as remote to them as any other moment in history. So she thinks about how the social, political, and cultural tensions of that era gave rise to fear, discrimination, and injustice, and she knows that these students have had many similar experiences in their own lives—bullies have inspired fear in them; others have discriminated against them because of their color, their body, their learning style, or their economic class; and they have been both the victim and the perpetrator of injustices. She introduces the civil rights unit by having students write about and then discuss their firsthand experiences with the tensions in their own lives that parallel the tensions of that time not so long ago.

When we are engaged spiritually, we feel connected to something outside of ourselves. We identify with the non-ego, as Steven Glazer (1999) points out: "One begins to feel *a part* of something rather than *apart* from something" (p. 82). We may discover deeper connections to ourselves, we may connect more closely with another human being or group of beings, or we may feel an affinity with a social or political cause. Rachel Kessler (1999), writing about the need to engage the heart in classrooms, identifies three kinds of deep connection students report and what we can do to cultivate these connections:

- *Through deep connection to the self,* students encounter a strength and richness that is the basis for developing the autonomy central to the adolescent journey, for discovering purpose, and for unlocking creativity. We can nourish this connection by giving students time for solitary reflection. Classroom exercises that encourage reflection and expression through writing or art also allow a student access to the inner self while in the midst of other people. Their total engrossment in such creative activities encourages students to discover and express their own feelings, values, and beliefs.
- *Connecting deeply to another person or to a meaningful group,* students discover the balm of belonging that soothes the alienation that fractures the identity of our youth and prevents them from contributing to our communities. To feel a sense of belonging at school, students must be part of the authentic community in the classroom. Many teachers regularly create this opportunity through morning meetings, weekly councils, or sharing circles offered in a context of ground rules that make vulnerability feel safe.
- *Connecting deeply to nature, to their lineage, or to a higher power,* students participate in a larger, ongoing source of meaning, a joy that gives them perspective, wisdom, and faith. . . . Out of connection grows compassion and passion—passion for people, for students' goals and dreams, for life itself. (pp. 51–52)

O'Reilley (2000) describes her yearlong spiritual journey tending sheep in a Minnesota agricultural barn, during which time she cared for the animals and a bond formed between herself and the sheep: "Tending sheep is a more symbiotic relationship than anything except perhaps motherhood. In some odd way I need these sheep to feel wholly myself" (p. 34). It is not far-fetched to read her story of tending sheep as a metaphor for teaching students and, by extension, to think of the classroom as a sacred place where connectedness is orchestrated through such activities as noted above from Kessler (1999)—morning meetings, weekly councils, and sharing circles. The drive for connectedness is natural and felt by everyone: its absence leads to a range of personal and interpersonal dysfunctions (narcissism, greed, profound loneliness, etc.). Palmer (1998/1999) cites the study of history as a spiritual event that shows us that "we are profoundly connected to the past in ways we may not even understand." Palmer writes that we can "evoke the spirituality of any discipline by teaching in ways that allow the 'big story' told by the discipline to intersect with the 'little story' of the student's life. Doing so not only brings up personal possibilities for connectedness but also helps students learn the discipline more deeply" (p. 9).

A moving example of little story/big story intersection appears in *In the Deep Heart's Core* (2003), Michael Johnston's compelling memoir about teaching high school English in Greenville, Mississippi, in 1997–98. Worried that one of his students, Larry, is ruining his life by running with a gang and by being disruptive in class, he invites the young man to play chess one afternoon rather than sleep through detention as he usually does. As the boy learns chess moves, Johnston talks about the game as a set of "golden rules":

> The first is you cannot survive without a plan, and in order to have a plan you must always think three steps ahead of where you are. . . . The second rule has to do with protecting yourself as you try to reach that goal. The second rule is this: Every action has a consequence, even if you don't see those consequences right away.

Johnston observes Larry's physical discomfort as he begins to recognize the relevance to his own life. Larry's unhealthy choices parallel choices other gang members make, with their inevitable loneliness certain to become his one day:

> I want to help you understand that every move you make without thinking puts you deeper in trouble, just like chess. If you just keep

drifting through each day not thinking about tomorrow, you're going to get eaten up. A chessboard has only thirty-two pieces on it, sixteen pieces for you and sixteen against you, and already you can see how tricky it is, how easy it is to get careless and make a stupid choice. Greenville has forty-five thousand people in it, and you can't just look at the colors and figure out who's for you and who's against you. That means it's that much more complicated, it's that much easier to get careless and make a stupid choice.

When you do things like getting thrown out of class every day, getting into fights, failing classes, you're making bad choices, you're not thinking about the consequences. If you clown around today, you miss the lesson, then you miss the assignment, then when the test comes around, you've never seen the stuff before, and you probably fail it. That cycle repeats itself until the next thing you know you're left like your friend Anthony, twenty years old and still in the tenth grade with nowhere to go. You're there because you weren't thinking about how every action has a consequence. (pp. 93–95)

This teacher challenged his student to rethink his connectedness to a group (gangs) while urging him to consider a healthier social identification. For Larry, the chess game became a vehicle that brought about new and compelling learning.

#3: COMPASSION

When Ms. James teaches argumentative writing to college students, the first thing she encounters is her students' learned habit of seeing every argument as having just two sides: "My side and the side of all the other dumb people who foolishly disagree with me" as one put it. Goodness here, evil there. Health versus illness. Success versus failure. She tries to help the students see that not everything has only two sides, that some (most) things have many sides—and plenty of uncomfortable grey areas. By college age, some students are intellectually ready for such multiplicity. But not all. Ms. James has to teach them how to become sympathetic with those people, ideologies, viewpoints, and values that seem alien to them at first glance. She has to convince them that their arguments become stronger when they can enter emotionally and intellectually into the minds and hearts of those with whom they disagree. In other words, she has to teach them intellectual compassion.

When her students prepare their arguments, they complete the graphic organizer called "Think in Threes" (Burke, 2002), in which they must move beyond polarized thinking (e.g., something is good or bad, right or wrong, etc.) by thinking about a topic from more than their single perspective. They have to enter into the minds and values of others, see issues from other points of view, understand how others think, and write from that broader point of view. Thus, the student who at first argues for reduced parking fees on campus based on his perspective as a student with a limited budget might, through the graphic organizer, see his proposal through the eyes of administrators trying to balance the campus budget, campus planners trying to conserve space, and students whose bus passes are subsidized by those very parking fees. He would then have to write with compassion for other views while still espousing his own.

Understanding how others think helps students develop intellectual compassion, and understanding how others feel helps students develop emotional compassion. In both cases, students become *attuned* to the thinking and feeling of others. Psychologist Daniel Goleman, author of *Emotional Intelligence* (1995), considers attunement key to successful emotional intelligence—and emotional intelligence, as we know, is key to a successful life in one's social world:

> Teamwork, open lines of communication, cooperation, listening, and speaking one's mind—rudiments of social intelligence . . . combine with individual emotional competencies—being attuned to the feelings of those we deal with, being able to handle disagreements so they do not escalate, having the ability to get into flow states while doing our work. (pp. 148–149)

Although compassion may not appear on the department or district list of expected student competencies, and though it may not show up on teachers' syllabi as a course goal, it is, nonetheless, an essential part of a holistic approach to engaging the hearts of students. Compassionate acts result from the practice of mindfulness and from the experience of connectedness. That is, when we practice mindfulness, we connect with something or someone other than ourselves. In doing so, we have the opportunity to become compassionate because we pay attention to *others.* In the vignette involving Michael Johnston and Larry, for instance, the teacher noticed his student's unhealthy life choices, imagined alternative connections Larry might make, and, out of compassion for a life most certainly headed for disaster, intervened.

I have separated spiritual engagement from neurological engagement so that readers can better grasp the parts that make up the whole, while still holding to the idea that engagement in learning *is* a whole. It is easy to see that mindfulness, as a heart-based phenomenon, is key to the brain-based search for patterns of meaning—one has to look closely in order to find meaning. Likewise, the heart-based need for finding connectedness and developing compassion necessarily involves the emotional drive of the brain—one has to feel for others in order to enter into their thoughts, values, and feelings. For who is to say when a neurologically charged moment of learning is *not* spiritual? Or when a compelling instant of compassionate recognition is *not* neurological? Engagement is neither purely neurological nor purely spiritual: It is both. As long as the mystery of who we are and what makes us *us* exists, we ought to view ourselves as both complex systems of electrochemical cells *and* as unpredictable, mysterious-wondrous creatures.

Engagement and Instructional Practice

Thinking about brain- and heart-based engagement as flow helps us make decisions about approaches and techniques when we plan instruction. Engagement is not the only thing we need to think about, to be sure, but it is high on the list. "Will X 'work'?" often hinges on whether we believe X will get students excited, hold their attention, and impact achievement. Reflective teachers weigh the value of teaching practices as they monitor the impact of those practices. When they learn from their students that engagement is high, they try to figure out just why it's so high; when they learn from their students that engagement is lacking, they try to figure out what's wrong.

If we consider engagement from the dual perspectives of engaged brains and engaged hearts, our instructional decision making will align with empirically validated "natural" ways of learning (brain-based) as well as with experientially validated "natural" ways of learning (heart-based). In doing so, we will be more able to understand why one approach "works" and another doesn't. We will begin to value some approaches over others for how well they "fit" with what we understand about how brains and hearts operate in flow states. Most of us, I believe, are realists who know that it is difficult for all our students to be thoroughly engaged all the time, but we are also idealists who know that aiming for the best in engaged learning—flow states—will take most of our students to some point along the spectrum of engagement below, from being unengaged (short vertical lines) to becoming optimally engaged (longer vertical lines) learners.

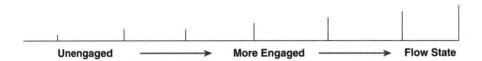

While our ultimate goal will be to bring students to flow states, moving anywhere to the right of unengaged will be movement in the right direction. Thus, our decisions about teaching and learning—everything from classroom geography to classroom discourse—become informed, deliberative decisions aimed at increasing engagement.

DECISIONS ABOUT ENGAGED LEARNING

How might we envision such informed, deliberative decision making? How might we synthesize brain-based learning with heart-based learning so that we can consider teaching practices for the extent to which they may engage learners? How might we predict the degree of flow our students will experience before we adopt practices or while we are revising them?

Let us examine predictability by posing questions that ask if a particular teaching approach may affect student engagement and how it might do so. We will consider these two questions with regard to both brain-based findings and heart-based elements. A caution: You can easily become overwhelmed by these questions if you think you need to consider all of them when planning teaching. As I discuss later, that is not the point. Rather, the point is that you should consider questions selectively, maybe one at a time, maybe more, as you become more sensitive to teaching for engaged brains and engaged hearts. To see what I mean, take just one question and apply it to a lesson you are preparing. See where the question leads you in your planning. Think of each question as a camera zoom lens: Through this lens, you zero in on particular aspects of lessons for the potential they hold for engaging students' brains and hearts. Then think of the combination of all the questions as a zoom-out, wide-angle lens that provides a way of thinking about the teaching of any subject matter.

Brain Decisions

From the perspective of the human brain, we know that engagement is more likely to occur when the brain is neurologically active. *An active brain searches for meaning by making synaptic connections.* If it is *not* making connections, it is *not* engaged. If the brain is making more elaborate connections, it is more engaged. It is that simple—and that complex. Connections may be between what is already in the brain (prior knowledge) and something new. Connections may also be between what at first seem to be disparate bits of information that later become coherent, such as when we listen to a speech or read an essay and, suddenly, in our brains, a theme emerges. (Actually, though it seems sudden, our brains were actively putting two and two together all along.) Some call this phenomenon *pattern discrimination*, like using visual clues to find Waldo in the Where's Waldo? puzzles. Connections can also be made when brains eliminate old connections because new information brings about a change in understanding, such as when emotional blocks begin to disappear as one "learns to like" something that was once disliked, or when one overcomes fear, such as working through test anxiety. When we think about how our instructional practices might *engage the brain in making connections*, we could ask the following questions as a way of predicting engagement:

- In what ways would this practice involve students in meaningful searches whereby they would make connections?
- What kinds of connections might they be making? For example, are students being introduced to new concepts in ways that relate those concepts to prior knowledge or experience?
- Are they going to make these connections themselves, or is someone else (a teacher) going to make the connections for them?
- Are students involved in constructing their own understanding of learning, or is the teacher or the textbook constructing it for them?
- How are their brains being directed to pay attention to some things while ignoring others?
- Are students being presented with an opportunity to make order out of apparent chaos?
- Are multiple memory pathways being called into play? Which ones?

We also know that *actively involved brains have strong emotions driving them.* The relationship between emotions and cognition is strong enough for us to plan lessons that have some kind of emotional import. Some teachers have practices with inherently emotional dimensions to them, such as class competitions and topical issues; others manufacture emotional import, such as posing emotional dilemmas when previewing a work of fiction to a class or presenting their own scientific wonderings and passionate curiosities before introducing a lab experiment. Further, we know from brain research that social activity has an emotional-cognitive dimension. Therefore, in predicting engagement based on emotional and social-emotional dimensions, we must ask, generally, *how are emotions being called into play?* That general question may take such specific forms as the following:

- How are students socially involved with one another in meaningful tasks? What is the ratio of meaningful individual tasks to meaningful group tasks?
- How might this practice build confidence in students who lack it in skill areas, such as reading a difficult text, understanding a math problem, or writing about science?
- How might this practice counteract learned helplessness? That is, how might it prove to students that they can achieve, can do better than they think? How will students' perceived or real weaknesses be addressed?
- Are students involved in making value decisions they care about or are emotionally involved with?
- How might students feel during this activity? How might they feel after?

Finally, we know that *engaged brains engender mind-body states* in which students experience *relaxed alertness*—they are comfortable, not threatened; appropriately stressed by challenge, not by fear; driven by internal curiosity, not by external compulsion. In optimal mind-body states, students are transported beyond their comfort zones by the learning, eager to take on more challenge because they feel safe and because they want to find out more—for example, How does this story end? What did the French Resistance do behind the lines? What will readers think if my memoir tells the truth about what really happened? If we want to promote engaged *bodyminds*, we should examine our plans for the *degree* to which we think they may bring about (or prevent) *mind-body states*:

- What in the activity is likely to help students experience relaxed alertness?
- What might threaten them to a point of causing the brain to downshift?
- Is the challenge on par with the student's level of skill, such that the goal seems reachable?
- Are there tensions that will likely move the learner deeper into learning or further toward solving a problem?
- Can we anticipate forms of cognitive dissonance—for example, paradoxes, contradictions, and alternative ways of viewing something—that challenge thinking?

- Does the practice encourage *intellectual playfulness* and experimentation, opportunities to put forth new ideas and encounter the unexpected?

Heart Decisions

From the perspective of the human heart, engagement is more likely when learners are involved in *mindful* activities. They may become more mindful by attending to their inner lives and by paying close attention to what is happening "in here." They may also form a relationship with their immediate external environment by paying attention to what is happening "out there." In predicting the engagement potential of *teaching practices to encourage mindfulness*, we may ask the following:

- Will students be called upon to make close observations—paying attention to details by looking closely, listening carefully, feeling fully?
- Will they be expected to name what they see, hear, feel, and so on?
- Will students be able to focus closely upon the present, encouraged to filter out intruding worries and fears? In the teaching practice called "guided imagery," for example, students are asked to suspend their normal flows of thought momentarily as they imagine themselves in a fictional place and time.

Spiritually engaged learners know that they are not alone in the world, that their hearts are connected with something or someone beyond themselves. This sense of *unity* works against the feelings of separation so prevalent in the world and against the sense of loneliness many students feel—in spite of cell phones and instant messaging. Unity creates hope as learners see that their lives have greater value because they are connected to something beyond themselves. Thus, when O'Reilley (2000) says that tending sheep makes her "feel wholly myself" (p. 289), she means that entering into spiritual unity with animals is a way of revaluing her self. The same is true for many of our students whose closeness to their pets has a spiritually uplifting dimension. As we think about how our teaching practices may promote *spiritual unity*, we can use the following predictive questions as a guide:

- How will students have opportunity to make deeper connections with themselves—for example, their values, ethics, morals, and beliefs?
- How will students have authentic encounters with others' values, ethics, morals, ideas, and ways of thinking?

- How will they be able to see that the little stories of their lives are related to the big stories of history, philosophy, literature, scientific inquiry, and the like?

When we become aware of our interdependence with others—when we become attuned—we experience compassion. When we are compassionate, we attune ourselves to the joys and sufferings of others; we take in opposing viewpoints in order to truly understand others. Learners can experience emotional compassion as well as intellectual compassion, and we can interrogate teaching practices accordingly:

- How will students become attuned to the lives of others (e.g., peers, fictional characters, historical or current people)?
- How will students gain insight into the real social-emotional lives of peers as well as of those people beyond the classroom?
- How will they experience the values and ways of thinking of those people with whom they disagree or with whom they have little understanding?

Flow State Decisions

The neurological and spiritual foundations of engaged learning discussed here are complemented by the primary research done on flow states. Reports by people who have experienced flow states always have brain- and heart-based dimensions to them, as seen in Chapter 1. We can mesh flow research with brain- and heart-based foundations to examine teaching practices. In his extensive research on flow, Csikszentmihalyi (1990a) finds five "conditions" that are common to flow states:

- Goals are clear.
- Feedback on our performance is immediate and relevant to our performance.
- There is balance between the level of challenge inherent in an activity and our ability to meet the challenge.
- We can concentrate on the activity.
- We enjoy the activity for its own sake. (paraphrased from p. 72)

I'll recast these conditions into questions that are useful in examining teaching practices:

- Do students have *clear goals* in this lesson? Can they articulate these goals themselves such that they know why they are engaging in a learning activity? I heard a student say recently, "I get what I'm supposed to do, but I don't get why I'm doing it." As a teacher, you may be challenged by questions like this, and you may even think students shouldn't be asking such things, but wouldn't classrooms be better places (i.e., more humane) if students knew why they spend their time as they do?

- How will students get *immediate feedback* that is relevant to their performance? Too often, feedback comes in summative forms—at the very end of an activity, much later, or not at all. Think of quizzes and exams. And so this question asks what mechanisms will be in place to provide *feedback-in-action* as opposed to *feedback-after-action*. Think of "exit cards," on which students jot down lingering questions before leaving the classroom; "in-class journals" in which students write what they understand or don't understand at designated times *during* a lesson; and "buddy checks," during which time students discuss their evolving understanding of a lesson with one another until they agree.

- How can we know if individual students' *skills are commensurate* with the challenge inherent in an activity? How will students not feel defeated because challenge exceeds skills or not become bored because talent exceeds challenge?

- Will students have opportunity to *concentrate* on the task at hand? What will have to change in order for concentration to become optimal?

- What are the chances of students coming to *enjoy* the activity for its own sake? What do you think they will really enjoy? Why that over the rest?

In short, we can consider prospective teaching practices through the engagement lens, asking questions, while planning, that bear on brain- and heart-based principles as well as on the conditions of flow. A single classroom teacher cannot possibly attend to all these questions when making important decisions about teaching and learning. There is just too much to keep in mind at once. But that is not the point. The questions are not to be taken as a list, wherein each must be checked off the way NASA might check off equipment prior to a launch.

A WAY OF THINKING

What we are after here is a way of thinking about scientifically and humanistically sound teaching. You might use one part of the theory at one time, perhaps interrogating a potential practice with a subset of questions like those on making synaptic connections or those on building compassion. Once you have that part integrated into your ways of thinking about practice, you might focus on another as you build, over time, greater familiarity with holistic engagement. Or let's say you're good about planning lessons that promote compassion, but you notice that that same lesson lacks multiple memory pathways; you wonder if that absence accounts for low student engagement, and so you redesign the lesson to include alternative learning pathways. That's all you do—for now.

As you use the questions to plan and revise instruction, you understand better the natural processes of engagement. Over time, this growing understanding becomes a way of thinking about teaching. With it, you increase your ability to make planning decisions with greater scientific and humanistic integrity, and you amend lessons as you use the questioning lens to "read" your students' degrees of engagement.

We need all the integrity, knowledge, and confidence we can get in order to be the sources of power *ourselves*, in order for us to be informed decision makers in league with science and with spiritual traditions. It is, in a word, our form of *connectedness*. To this end, in Part II, you will see how teaching based on such informed decision making can create and sustain engaged learning in diverse school settings.

PART II

Teaching for Engaged Learning

Engaged learning moves, shakes, and changes people. For American poet Emily Dickinson, reading poetry was a visceral experience vastly different from ordinary reading, as she explained to her biographer, Thomas Wentworth Higginson (1891): "If I read a book and it makes my whole body so cold no fire can ever warm me, I know that is poetry. If I feel physically as if the top of my head were taken off, I know that is poetry. These are the only ways I know it. Is there any other way?" (1891).

Engaged learning takes people on profound mind adventures. For Richard Sterling (2005), recent executive director of the National Writing Project, having access to many sources of information at one time when problem solving takes him deeper into learning. It is a dynamic, intellectual experience. Explaining that his "grasshopper mind," as his teachers called it, often got him into trouble at school, he later learned that "organized" learning (i.e., linear learning, one source at a time) does not lead him as quickly or compellingly into the quest for knowledge: "I love information from multiple sources. I like putting seemingly disparate things together. . . . Engagement always resulted when I could follow many paths to the goal." It should come as no surprise that the advent of the Internet made him "one happy person" who works with "three or four windows open at the same time, and a TV news channel on mute with two or three crawls at the bottom of the screen."

Engaged learning brings about understanding. Like Dickinson and Sterling, we all have known the "aha" experience of compelling learning—those moments when we went below the surface of things to a deeper understanding. We may have been reading intensely and discovered suddenly a depth to the passage that we did not see previously, which made the reading a whole new experience. We may have studied a painting that we have seen scores of times but this time went beyond color and texture to lines, understanding the work as we never had before.

Engaged learning also changes previous understanding. I can, for example, read a statement that catches my interest. But when I *transcribe* that statement, actually write it out, something in the eye-hand-brain process of transcribing brings me closer to the style or the meaning of the piece that I did not catch the first, second, or third time around. I learn more; I admire more. So it is that many writers begin their writing lives by imitating the style of other writers.

Engaged learning brings immense pleasure. For Dickinson, it was her profound love for language; for Sterling, his insatiable drive for knowledge; for me, a habit of mind Ray (1999) calls "reading like a writer" to learn how to improve my own writing style. Engaged learning builds on, and then extends beyond, what brain researchers Caine and Caine (1997) describe as the two types of knowledge gained in schooling:

- *Surface knowledge:* Often what results from rote learning, surface knowledge may consist of isolated facts (such as what we find in textbooks), narrow skills (such as identifying parts of speech), or mnemonic devices (such as acronyms for memorizing steps in a procedure). Useful for practical purposes such as downloading from an Internet site or changing a tire, surface knowledge doesn't take one very far into complex thinking.
- *Technical, or scholastic, knowledge:* Borrowing from Gardener (1991), Caine and Caine (1997) describe technical knowledge as the "ideas, principles, and procedures that are traditionally regarded as the core content of any subject or discipline." While valued for its abstract intellectual power, technical knowledge too often lacks "a quality that makes it available for solving real problems or for dealing with complex situations . . . and lacks a grasp for practical application" (pp. 110–111), such as when a person can identify a psychological theory but is challenged to apply the theory to real people or when our students memorize textbook "facts" but do not move beyond them as isolated nuggets of information.

Unfortunately, much of schooling has superficial knowledge as its primary focus, which explains why so many students can recite facts and recall bits of information but struggle to integrate and apply what they remember. If we want to inculcate meaning and understanding rather than just surface knowledge, we must concern ourselves with the two types of meaning Caine and Caine (1997) identify as *meaning rich:*

- *Deep meaning* motivates by personal drives for genuine understanding. "Deep meanings are the source of most intrinsic motivation. They are the source of our reasons to keep going even when we do not understand. Thus, deep meaning is an initial source of energy that spurs inquiry" (p. 112) and that makes genuine learning stick.
- *Felt meaning* complements intellectual understanding by adding the emotional component. It is "the coming together of thoughts and ideas and senses and impressions and emotions, something like a chemical reaction." As I discussed in Part I, powerful emotions drive optimal learning, such that "any in-depth understanding of any subject, skill, or domain requires some integration of thought and feeling." (p. 113)

Engaged learning consists of both kinds of knowledge and both kinds of meaning. It relies on surface and technical knowledge to get to the higher-order work of developing deep meaning and felt meaning. What too often happens in school, however, is that learning stops with surface and technical knowledge, falling short of engaged learning—for a variety of reasons ranging from evaluation (where what is tested depends on what *can* be tested) to pressure to cover the curriculum, and to misguided perceptions of what some students need (e.g., the belief that teacher-dominated rote instruction is essential in urban schools or with English language learners). Why engaged learning is so often missing is a complex and multi-faceted question and is beyond my purpose here, however important, indeed essential, such a discussion has been (see Barell, 2003; Costa, 2001; Schmoker, 2006, 2007).

In keeping with my purpose here, in this part of the book, I look more closely at what actually happens in classrooms. The chapters that follow take up, each in its turn, common activities that give rise to engaged learning across the subjects and levels, K–16.

Chapter 5, "Modeling Engaged Learning," presents three complementary modeling practices: *modeling habits of mind, modeling habits of the heart,* and *modeling work habits.* Readers ought to find this chapter helpful in planning demonstration teaching.

Chapter 6, "Using Words That Support Engaged Learning," examines the ways in which we and our students talk to and with one another, with particular focus on how language itself fosters engaged learning. Here, readers will be encouraged to become more deliberative in the words they choose in their teaching, including the words they choose to talk about students' intelligence.

Chapter 7, "Using Discussions to Engage Learners," continues the examination of classroom talk by considering ideas, questions, silence, and the dynamics of discussion that engage students. Those of us who teach by discussion will learn effective ways to help students participate as active partners in classroom discussions.

Chapter 8, "Supporting Engaged Readers," examines school-sponsored reading from the perspective of a student and presents reading from a "trinal" viewpoint—what readers need before, during, and after reading. The numerous strategies in this chapter will guide readers in thinking about how to teach reading across the curriculum.

Chapter 9, "Supporting Engaged Writers," contrasts writing to prove learning with writing to promote learning. Here, the focus is on the purposes, audiences, and forms of writing to support learning. Like Chapter 8, this chapter guides readers in the ways they can use writing to learn across the curriculum.

Chapter 10, "Promoting Engagement Through Memory Pathways," looks at memory pathways in the brain and ways to support students' learning and long-term memory. Readers of this chapter will learn how nonverbal memory pathways can provide alternatives to the primary (and least efficient) memory pathway characteristic of most schools—the semantic pathway.

Slicing the classroom pie into different classroom activities like this risks isolating activities that naturally must be fully and thoughtfully integrated. Nonetheless, each activity will be examined separately in order to come to some understanding of how just that activity alone can promote engaged learning. One can then imagine how much greater engagement in learning is possible when all classroom activities, not just one, are geared toward flow experiences through *wholesight* instructional planning, as discussed in the Afterword.

Another point about the upcoming chapters: Throughout, you'll see references to research on classroom practices. How do we know that what we do not only helps students learn better but also actually helps them achieve more in school? This is a question that we ought to be able to answer with confidence. Accordingly, the instructional practices presented in Part II have been proved by controlled studies to positively affect student academic achievement, and I asterisk the research studies that answer the *Does It Work?* question in each chapter. So, for example, when you read about modeling, you can go to Langer (2002*); Schoenbach, Greenleaf, Cziko, and Hurwitz (1999*); or Olson and Land (2007*) for a more in-depth understanding of how teacher demonstration influences achievement. They are not all the possible instructional practices that contribute to flow, to be sure. That they are representative practices of engaged learning *and* proven to affect achievement makes them all the more powerful.

Finally, it must be noted that many other factors affect engaged learning in addition to the activities discussed in the following chapters. For example, the emotional climate of the classroom, physical condition of the school, positive teacher–student relationships, interest level of curriculum materials, cultural histories of the students, inclusion of English language learners and mainstreamed special populations, availability of texts and materials—the list goes on. We could just start with *interesting* texts and materials and then go on to making them available! Suffice it to say that I am not unaware of the larger dynamics, conditions, and complexities inherent in the work of creating engaging communities of learners, and I have more to say about this in the Afterword. In an ideal world, everything would be done at once, of course, but in the real world, most of us can focus on just a few factors in the short term, with the goal of increasing or changing engaging instructional practices in the long term.

Modeling
Engaged Learning

At this school, eleventh-grade American History is a yearlong course. For months, Mr. Ernhart, the teacher, has reminded his students of their culminating assignment in the course—a research paper on any course topic of their choice. Until now, however, his students have given the assignment little thought. On this April day, Mr. Ernhart and his class begin the research paper unit:

"So, the topic is your choice, but you need my approval before you start working on the research. This paper should be eight pages, typed and double spaced, with at least four references, in proper bibliographic form."

Jimmy groans. "Mr. E., eight pages?"

"Yes, but the topic is up to you; you have some choice on that."

In the back row, Sandy raises her hand. "Mr. E., how are we supposed to decide on a topic? I mean, like, what's a good topic?"

"Anything you're interested in learning more about, or anything you wonder about, Sandy."

She rolls her eyes. "Can't you just give us one, Mr. E.? I hate choosing topics."

Mr. Ernhart studies her for a moment and feels the familiar resistance set in. He thinks, "It happens every year with the juniors. But this research paper is required in the junior curriculum, and they need to learn to do independent research if any of them plans to go to college. I know these kids will become more interested in their research if they can latch onto a good topic."

"Look everyone," he says raising his voice, "this is your opportunity to follow your interests in a history topic. I'm not gonna dictate topics to you. Choose a war or an election, an important crisis, something that interests you."

Jimmy glances across the aisle at Manuel, who raises his hand. "How much time do we have to work on this research paper, sir?"

"Three weeks, final draft due May 16. You'll have class time to work on it—in the library, on the Internet, and so forth. That's enough time. Look, I told you guys that a research paper would be required in this class way last September, and I've mentioned it quite a few times since. I guess you forgot about it until today! For many of you, doing a good job on the paper will raise your grade."

"Guess we did forget," mutters Manuel; others sitting near him slouch in their seats.

Research papers are a mainstay in American schools and colleges. The ability to investigate a subject using source materials, examine it critically, and consolidate the results of that search into a product is an important lifelong set of academic skills. But the *Research Paper*, as it is taught in most settings, is seen by most students as a dull affair. When Mr. Ernhart reminds them of the research paper, learned helplessness, likely derived from an academic history of completing uninteresting research projects like this one, sets in. This teacher gives much initial attention to formal requirements—how long the paper must be, when it's due, the number of references, the impact on course grade, and so on. This focus on formal properties of the research reinforces the idea of *Research Paper* held by his students—a perfunctory rite of passage through the junior year.

Mr. Ernhart's topic choice seems to be a good teaching practice aimed at making the assignment interesting through personal selection. But these students resist choice because of the way it is presented. Clearly something is wrong, for their minds are not engaged. Neither are their hearts.

In terms of engagement, Mr. Ernhart's hunch is correct: Students may well find the research meaningful if they can get motivated to do it in the first place. So the real problem here is not what students might do once they get into the research. The real problem is getting them *to* that point. In terms of instructional practice, this teacher has not invited their curiosity, and curiosity is what drives research in the first place.

Mr. Ernhart would like his students to get excited about doing historical research; that's why he leaves the topic open to their own choosing. But given the somber invitation he has extended, excitement hardly seems possible to them at this early stage—because they just are not connected to the assignment. Nor is there much likelihood that students will enjoy doing the research. In order for that to happen, Mr. Ernhart would have to change his introduction to the research project and align that with a vision of the engaged researcher, starting with himself.

As he stands before his students, Mr. Ernhart is a living model of the historian. All teachers represent their respective disciplines—the art teacher represents the world of artists; the language arts teacher the writer and reader; the science teacher, the world of scientific inquiry; and so on. As a history teacher, Mr. Ernhart is to his students a teacher and a historian—he has multiple opportunities to model for his young historians what it means to do historical research.

But in the vignette, what *does* he model? For one thing, he models *the reasons historians do research,* but this scene enacts a dubious reason: Historical research is driven by teachers' assignments. While it is true that many assignments become the artificial impetus for doing research in many academic settings, that is not the reason for genuinely engaged research. Take out the external force and what do you have left? Nothing, or in Mr. Ernhart's mind, the hope that engagement will come eventually. What we are after is not externally imposed motivation, but internally driven motivation—for that lays the groundwork for engaged research. While he cannot ignore the fact that the curriculum demands that students conduct research, he is not obligated to make that mandate the central focus when inviting his students to begin the research process. Mr. Ernhart needs to focus on genuine motivation.

He also models the values of the history researcher that identify what is most important in conducting historical research. In this vignette, what seem most valued are the products of that research—length, appearance, and references. If the value were to be placed on the research process, then we would likely see other features of research highlighted, such as asking a good question, valuing one type of research data over another (e.g., textbook facts versus original historical documents), and coming to one's own conclusions about historical events.

In short, like all teachers, Mr. Ernhart represents that group of people students know as historians, readers, mathematicians, writers, economists, and the like. As such, he has unlimited opportunities to model for his students the real wonderments historians have that drive their curiosity, the real doubts they may have at times, and the real ways they go about researching.

TEACHER MODELING

For many teachers, *modeling* means showing students how to complete some task—for example, set up a lab experiment, write an introductory paragraph, or give a dramatic reading—that students are then expected to complete themselves. Engaged modeling goes much further than merely completing a task, for, in it, we share our ways of thinking and feeling so that students engage with ideas, dilemmas, and intellectual, emotional, and ethical challenges.

Kohn (2004) proposes that teachers practice modeling as a way of focusing students' attention on the processes as well as the products of learning. In this model, teachers show how they go about the processes of thinking and doing, and the feelings that go with both. They draw students' attention to the real decisions people make while engaged in some activity (such as doing historical research, writing, reading, or solving a math problem). At these moments, Kohn argues, we have an opportunity to "let children know how we think (and feel) our way through similar dilemmas by describing to them the factors that we consider in making such decisions: the relevance of our previous experiences, the principles from which we're operating, and all the thoughts and emotions that we take into account" (p. 186). Modeling takes students "backstage" to the gray areas. Kohn writes that

> It's very much like writing—or conducting an authentic science experiment—in front of them. They're able to experience what happens before (or behind) the ethical decisions that adults make, the essays they publish, and the scientific principles they discover—all of which are usually presented to children as so many *faits accomplis.* (p. 186)

In demystifying the activity, Kohn says, "we demystify the people engaged in the activity." This, he says, is "authentic teaching" (p. 186), the kind that invites students into learning communities where people savor the brain and heart work necessary for academic success.

Modeling Habits of Mind and Heart

Habits of mind and heart are the intellectual and emotional dispositions people hold privately and exhibit publicly through their actions. Habits of mind might include artistic perspective taking, as when the art teacher shares her aesthetic perspective on an art object; analytical problem solving, as when the writing teacher models how she analyzes her audience when constructing an argumentative essay; and transference, as when the history teacher models how he applies the lessons of history to the problems of today. We model our habits of the heart when we show compassion to people with whom we disagree, when we comfortably accept challenges to our own assumptions, and when we persevere in the face of doubt.

In classrooms where we practice engaged modeling, our habits of mind and heart support one another. Barell's (1995) integrative (i.e., brain and heart) approach to teaching called "teaching for thoughtfulness" specifies the "characteristics of thoughtful people," all of which can be read as core habits of mind and heart:

- They have confidence in problem-solving abilities.
- They persist.
- They control their own impulsivity and deliberate appropriately.
- They are open to others' ideas.
- They cooperate with others in solving problems.
- They listen.
- They are empathetic.
- They tolerate ambiguity and work toward resolving complex issues.
- They approach problems from a variety of perspectives.
- They research problems thoroughly.
- They relate prior experience to current problems and make multiple connections.
- They are open to many different solutions and evidence that may contradict favored points of view.
- They pose what-if questions, challenging assumptions and playing with variables.
- They can draw reasonable conclusions.
- They are reflective; they plan, monitor, and evaluate their thinking.
- They are able to transfer concepts and skills from one situation to another.
- They are curious and wonder about the world. They ask "good questions." (p. 47)

If we plan lessons with an eye toward modeling such habits, we teach *ourselves* as much as we teach our subjects. One of the best examples of teachers who teach themselves appears in Mike Rose's (1989) *Lives on the Boundary*, where Mr. Johnson, his Loyola University philosophy professor, models habits of mind and heart when teaching the history of ideas:

> As he laid out his history of ideas, Mr. Johnson would consider aloud the particular philosophical issue involved, so we didn't, for example, just get an outline of what Hegel believed, but we watched and listened as Don Johnson reasoned like Hegel and then raised his own questions about the Hegelian scheme. He was a working philosopher, and he was thinking out loud in front of us. (p. 49)

Modeling dialectical reasoning and intellectual skepticism, Mr. Johnson showed students like Rose intellectual persistence, reflective thinking, and confidence in his ability to penetrate difficult texts. Like many of the students we face daily, Rose was challenged by the difficulty of the reading: "I was reading words but not understanding text. I was the human incarnation of language-recognition computer programs: able to record the dictionary meanings of individual words but unable to generate any meaning out of them" (p. 50). However, over time and with more exposure to Mr. Johnson's demonstrated thinking strategies, Rose began to read and think like a philosopher:

> Mr. Johnson was helping me develop an ability to read difficult texts—I was learning how to reread critically, how to tease out definitions and basic arguments. And I was gaining confidence that if I stayed with material long enough and kept asking questions, I would get it. That assurance proved to be more valuable than any particular body of knowledge I learned that year. (p. 51)

Modeling thoughtfulness calls for us to demonstrate those habits of mind and heart that enable us to be successful in meeting our own academic challenges. We talk about a task's emotional demands: We articulate doubt as doubt arises, by saying "I'm not sure here, but . . ." or "I may make a mess of this, but here goes anyway" and "I know this sounds stupid, but maybe it'll get me going here." We reveal a tenacious engagement with such challenges, by saying things like "Wow. What an interesting contradiction this is turning out to be!" and "Now this is really puzzling. I love this kind of challenge!"

In other words, we talk about ourselves while we are in action, practicing audible *reflection-in-action*. But we also practice *audible reflection-on-action* (here, I borrow from the terms Donald Schoen, 1987, uses to describe reflective teaching) when we look back on a problem and talk about the process of solving or attempting to solve it. Thus we may say, "I didn't think I would ever get through that chapter, but when I took it paragraph by paragraph, it began to make more sense" and "Wow. That poem was tough. At first, I said to myself, 'What is going on here?' but when I just looked at the imagery, I started to see things coming together and I knew I was going to figure it out."

Modeling habits of mind and heart reflects a number of predictability decisions we make when thinking about instructional practice (see Chapter 4):

- *Mind:* It encourages curiosity, intellectual playfulness, and experimentation by showing these habits of mind at work.

- *Heart:* It helps students become attuned to the lives of others (the teacher) as they learn more about how another person approaches challenges.
- *Flow:* Because modeling engaged learning practices can break down global tasks into more manageable component parts, it helps students have clearer (i.e., more specific) goals for their academic tasks by working on one goal at a time, such as, in the example above, studying just the image patterns in a poem.

Modeling Work Habits

Habits of work are practical, and they include such skills as being thorough, setting clear goals, and monitoring progress. We can model such academic work habits as skimming a text for the big ideas, writing in a journal to explore thinking, and imagining a skeptical audience in order to enrich one's own perspective. In *The Students Are Watching Us: Schools and the Moral Contract*, Sizer and Sizer (1999) argue persuasively that "They watch us all the time. The students, that is. They listen to us, sometimes. They learn from all that watching and listening" (p. xvii). What they see, of course, are our work habits, our ways of presenting ourselves as people who practice what we profess:

> The biology teacher who, spring after spring, tracks the nesting patterns of red-winged blackbirds, dragging his students before dawn into a mosquito-infested swamp to watch and record the movements of the birds. The English teacher who writes poetry, shares it with her students, and not only teaches drama but directs student performances. The coach who keeps on top of her game, razor-sharp on new rules, plays, and practices and is always ready to share them. (p. 11)

Habits of mind and heart drive work habits, those actions we take to meet challenges, solve problems, and accomplish tasks. These are the concrete things we do that instantiate our habits of mind and heart. People's work habits differ, and some have better work habits than others and are consequently more successful than others. When we model our own work habits for students, we show, not *the* ways of getting work done, but *our* ways. We engage students momentarily in *our* ways of meeting the challenges of daily academic life, *our* problem-solving strategies, *our* ways of being strategic about our work. To illustrate, let us look more closely at three typical work habits that any of us can model.

Thinking

Students can't see us think, but we can still model thinking. I first learned about thinking habits from my father. He taught me important ways of thinking that helped me develop critical thinking. A machinist by trade with a first-rate practical intelligence, he could fix virtually anything that broke down at home. He was immensely patient and curious when it came to appliance repair, in particular, and he could systematically analyze those contrivances when they stopped working or started making odd noises. From him, I learned that the art of fixing mechanical devices calls for thoughtful study, tinkering, and saying "Hmm" a lot. So when he invited ten- or eleven-year-old me to examine, say, the toaster that had begun reducing bread to ashes, I sat beside him at his workbench, the malfunctioning toaster before us. I watched him stare a lot at the toaster, so I stared too. We peeked down into the inside coils, plugged it in and unplugged it, turned it upside down as crispy crumbs tumbled out, and then stared some more. Then, he posed questions out loud, sometimes acting as if I weren't even there. His questions smacked of scientific inquiry as they sought to weigh alternate hypotheses. A typical appliance repair session went like this:

"So what's wrong with the toaster?" he'd say.

"Burns the bread."

"What's wrong with that?"

"We don't like burned toast."

"I do."

"Well, but no one else but you likes it!"

"Well, that's true enough. Where do you think we should start then? Where did we start last time, with your mother's iron?"

"With the cord."

"Hmm. I was thinking about that iron, how the cord jiggled where it went into the casing, and that was exactly where the problem was. But does this one do that?"

I would check out the cord, especially where it went into the toaster casing. "Doesn't look like it," I would say (but he already knew what I would find).

"So maybe the problem isn't with the cord."

"Hmm," I'd say, "I wonder. Maybe the dial is broken."

"Could be," he would say, turning the dial, and then, talking out loud, to himself, "I notice that it heats up OK. See how it glows when we turn it on?"

"Yeah."

"So, if it's getting plenty of juice, then we can rule that out, right?"

I would grow restless, inevitably saying, "Why don't we just buy a new one?"

That I would inevitably regret saying, because that would give up on the whole challenge, which was, I came to realize many years later, the life skill he was really teaching. He would never comment on defeatist words like that.

Thus, the examination of the toaster would go, moving from one potential trouble spot to the other, with questions, speculations, and confirmations accompanying each step. He had his own ideas but wanted to know mine first, and he treated mine with dignity, no matter how far-fetched. By himself, he could have fixed the toaster in fifteen minutes, but he took an hour in order to teach me. I learned that when you think through mysterious problems, even bad ideas have exploratory value, but it is the carefully reasoned ones that moved us along toward understanding and repairing small appliances. Decades later, I still have the same work habits when I fix something around my home: I think and tinker, try this and that, hem and haw, and curse a few times, of course.

I have the same work habits when I encounter an academic thinking problem: I turn the problem around in my head, consider many perspectives; poke at it with mental probes, trying out a few avenues of exploration; form tentative hypotheses; try out the hypotheses, get feedback, and refine them. Like my father, I talk about these ways of thinking aloud, in class and in individual conferences with students, as I try to help them become more reflective about their own academic work habits. I'm confident, too, that modeling work habits helps student achievement: In Langer's (2002*) research on effective literacy instruction, for instance, teachers taught students "enabling strategies" for reading, writing, and thinking; through strategy modeling, teachers demonstrated for students how to think about school tasks, how to complete tasks, and how to reflect on their task performance.

Writing

"Good teachers show what they mean instead of telling," writes Donald Graves (1983, p. 277), referring to helping young writers in the classroom. "Think back," he writes. "When was the last time you observed another person write . . . When [students] see us write, they will see the middle of the process, the hidden ground, from the choice of topic to the final completion of the work" (p. 43). Similarly, writing advocate Katie Wood Ray (1999) urges teachers to model writing work habits so students will come to see them as authentic fellow writers:

> Students can see the real work of a real person in what their teacher says and does, and teaching is not seen as the performance of right answers that deserves applause. Students take to the teaching so differently when they see their teacher as being like them and like the writers they are trying to become. (p. 47)

Teachers who make their writing work habits visible to students not only demystify writing but also democratize the classroom, as Ray points out: "Either we can be walking, breathing, talking examples of all we advocate for our students, or we can have them sitting around wondering why we are trying to get them into something that we are obviously not into ourselves" (p. 98).

Teachers who model writing strategies also model habits of mind and heart: imagination in developing an angle on a topic, confidence in overcoming writing blocks, persistence in completing the writing task, pride in how the final product looks, and joy in sharing their writing with others. For example, a history teacher can show students how his particular interest in historical economic forces leads him to view historical events from the perspective of human greed: Thus, when he writes about history, he uses that lens to narrow the focus of his research, thereby showing how he develops an angle on a topic (an important writing skill in its own right). The science teacher can demonstrate for students how she evaluates the validity of competing scientific explanations, by showing students the ways she examines the types of evidence scientists use to support their claims; thus, she shows students that, as a science writer, she has to read like a scientist in order to write like a scientist. Finally, the English teacher can model how she revises a paper for her graduate course—describing the various ways *she* procrastinates and showing how *she* drafts from outlines and revises for organization, style, and grammar.

Reading

When we model reading work habits, we demonstrate how we ourselves read difficult texts. Social studies teachers, for example, teach by modeling how they read original source materials or history textbooks, making use of the rhetorical, formatting, and typographical cues to build

comprehension. Math teachers demonstrate how they read story problems, highlighting important mathematical details and grammatical con-
structions (e.g., similar to, different from, greater than/less than) as they
read aloud. And science teachers show students how they read challenging articles in science magazines, giving special attention to the ways
visual aides augment written passages.

Modeling reading habits by talking aloud while reading is known as
"think alouds" or "reading apprenticeships." When we conduct think
alouds, we verbalize the starts and stops in our growing understanding of
a text, the surges and the dead ends, the "aha" moments, and the familiar
urge to give up when the going gets tough. Think alouds democratize
reading strategies and promote emotional safety. When students feel
daunted by reading difficult texts and get to the point of giving up, or
when they read the words but lack the comprehension, their intellectually
and emotionally threatened brains *downshift* and their threatened hearts
give up. Reading apprenticeships, known to impact student achievement
(Schoenbach et al., 1999*), "make it safe for students to take risks in the
classroom community. After all, if the teacher—the master reader—is
willing to reveal his or her own confusion about a text, students who feel
confused won't feel so alone. More important, students will begin to see
that confusion is a natural state of being for all readers at various points
in their reading experience" (p. 123).

In reading apprenticeships, we make our otherwise invisible reading
processes visible, thereby teaching such critical thinking skills as problem
solving, classifying, and closely observing:

> One eleventh-grade English teacher introduces the kind of problem-
> solving strategies needed to make sense of a difficult literary text
> by reading aloud the first paragraph of "Wash," a short story by
> William Faulkner. As he reads, he also thinks aloud about the
> text. Students are asked to categorize his think alouds into five
> types of mental moves: picturing, questioning, summarizing,
> recalling, and clarifying. Similarly, a chemistry teacher thinks
> aloud as she demonstrates a laboratory procedure in front of her
> class, following instructions, making observations and careful
> descriptions, and drawing conclusions. These teachers draw
> students into the activity of consciously puzzling through texts
> and classroom activities. They begin the apprenticeship process
> by making thinking visible—and by making the confusions, false
> starts, and retracings that characterize reading for understand-
> ing an accepted part of classroom life. (Schoenbach et al., 1999,
> p. 123)

In addition to illuminating reading processes, think-aloud practices teach a range of academic skills. Science teachers can model how their thinking—as scientists—changes as they observe the natural world or as they note the chemical changes in a lab experiment. Math teachers can model their ways of ciphering—working their way through mathematical calculations or experimenting with different algorithms. Foreign language teachers can model their ways of translating using semantic, syntactic, and contextual cues. In all these instances, we make visible for learners our academic work habits, and in doing so, we demystify the processes of writing, reading, thinking, calculating, and the like.

When we incorporate work-habits modeling into instructional practice, we can become more predictive about the potential for engaged learning (see Chapter 4):

- *Mind*: Students are involved in social activities and they make connections between their own challenges and those of a trusted adult through mindful observation.
- *Heart*: Students experience people's (teachers) ways of thinking, with which they usually have little familiarity. They have opportunity to become attuned to another person.
- *Flow*: Students learn about goals and how goals drive their teachers' work habits and help them become strategic in meeting those goals.

HISTORY CLASS REVISITED

Let us return to the classroom scenario presented at the beginning of this chapter. While we may praise Mr. Ernhart for providing his students with the opportunity of deciding their research topics, we also see how much his practice of introducing the research paper involves the subtle threat of meeting formal requirements and the overt threat of grades. We also notice what is missing—why anyone would want to conduct academic research in the first place and, more specifically, why Mr. Ernhart himself, as a historian, would want to. Furthermore, just how would he go about deciding on a historical research topic himself?

Were Mr. Ernhart to think less about the research product and more about the research process, he could adopt teaching practices that represent the historian at work. He would begin by asking himself just what habits of mind and heart are characteristic of research historians. Referring to Barell's (1995) "Characteristics of Thoughtful Persons" (mentioned earlier), he would notice at least the following habits of mind:

- They research problems thoroughly.
- They approach problems from a variety of perspectives.
- They are able to transfer concepts from one situation to another.

He would also notice certain habits of the heart:

- They are curious and wonder about the world. They ask good questions.
- They persist.

Mr. Ernhart would plan his lesson with the intent of making such habits of mind and heart visible, and he would also plan to model his own work habits through his actions. He would share with his students a current wondering he has about a historical event, say Hitler's triumphant march into Paris in 1940. He would talk about how he's always been interested in knowing more about the moral dilemmas that that event provoked among a certain segment of the French population who were eventually to become German sympathizers. The discussion might go like this.

"I wonder," he ruminates aloud before his students, "about those people who were eventually to become German sympathizers. What must they have been thinking, to aid and abet an army they knew was determined to destroy their country? I mean, were they greedy people who saw an opportunity to make some money or protect what riches they had? Did they see sympathizing as a way of protecting themselves and their families? I know the facts of the German occupation of France, but I don't know about the inner lives of the French people."

Manuel raises his hand and asks, "Why do you want to know about them, sir?"

Mr. Ernhart pauses, thinks a bit, and responds, "That's a good question, one I've thought about too. This may sound weird, but one of the things I like about studying history is to imagine, 'What would I have done if I had lived back then?' You've heard the phrase 'history repeats itself' haven't you? Well, one thing that means is that people are people throughout the world and throughout time. And their actions, like going to war, are usually based on common human motives, like nationalism, greed, and fear. So I'm always interested in the human stories that are part of historical events, which is why I like to read historical biographies and autobiographies too—to learn about people's own stories back then. I like to put myself in their shoes."

"So what about those French turncoats, Mr. E.?" asks Sandy.

"Well, what if I had a big family and I was pretty wealthy?" he responds. "I wonder how I would have thought about it all. What would I have done? I mean, isn't family more important than country? And what if I were Jewish? That really makes it complicated from a moral perspective! Why might a Jewish person become a sympathizer, horrible as that may sound?

"Anyway," he continues, "that is how I think about doing research—on things that I wonder about, not just the facts of the historical event, though those are important too, but on the people who were affected by historical events. I have many wonderings about history, and that's why I'm a history teacher. I like doing research too because I get a chance to follow those wonderings, which

is what you have an opportunity to do too. But let's take some time, as much as we need, to help one another find good research topics for this assignment. Don't worry about how long it has to be or when it's due, not yet. Let's save that for the next few days; all we'll do now is help one another find a good topic and narrow it down so that you can really use it for this paper. I'm here to help, so let's get started."

You can detect a much different tone in this scenario as compared with the one at the start of the chapter. Mr. Ernhart's focus on himself as a curious historian invites students into seeing him as a real learner whose interest in history is driven by curiosity about the humans who lived it. He invites students into the "history club" by sharing his wonderings with them and by connecting the big stories of history with the little story of his own life ("What would I have done?"). He searches for and makes connections between the past and the present, and he notices compelling human dilemmas (my family or my country?). We would hope that his ways of thinking in this one segment of the class are consistent with his teaching practices throughout the rest of the course, such that his eagerness to speculate and inquire is apparent in his other teaching practices.

Finally, we would expect that, as part of his entire unit on the research paper, Mr. Ernhart would also model his work habits, demonstrating for his students how he would go about finding information on the French sympathizers, taking notes, weighing and documenting sources, drafting, revising, and so on. Knowing that his students may encounter some difficult reading during the course of their research, he may even use reading apprenticeship practices to show the strategies he uses to read challenging source materials.

As a history teacher, Mr. Ernhart represents himself to his students as a fellow researcher-thinker-writer-reader. He exudes a confidence that his students will succeed by inviting them to take the tiny first steps of success. He draws them into the history club through the back door, where real people like himself ask real questions and where real people take ownership over knowledge by personally appropriating it. Next, I look closely at how teachers like Mr. Ernhart talk about themselves and their students as serious, engaged, and successful learners of their subjects.

Using Words That Support Engaged Learning

Mrs. Burns's fifth graders are in the middle of a science unit on world habitats. The students have been working in small groups for days, each with their own habitat to research in preparation for their end-of-unit presentations to one another. As stated on their study guide worksheet, their presentation must have three parts: a physical description of the habitat, locations of the habitat on a world map, and examples of plants and animals living in the habitat. For extra credit, they can report on how animals adapt to conditions in the habitat.

Today, Mrs. Burns monitors groups in the learning resource center as they research their habitats. The Tropical Rain Forest group sits at a table, downloaded Web information, magazine articles, and books spread around them. Each student has a notebook in which to record information. Mrs. Burns sits with the group:

"So how is your work coming on the three parts of the study guide? Which one are you on, Andrea?"

Andrea flips to her assignment worksheet, her finger poised in the middle of the page. "Well," she begins, "we sorta skipped the first one about describing the rain forest and went to the second one about the animals and plants that live there, and we started listing all the animals there—monkeys, jaguars, snakes, um, we have them on our list here!"

"That's good," says Mrs. Burns. "Good to list them all like that. But you have a long way to go because there are a lot more animals in the rain forest than

just those three. Not that you have to have all of them down, but three is hardly a start. What other work have you done? Francisco?"

Francisco opens April Pulley Sayre's book Tropical Rain Forests *and shows his teacher a picture. "See, Mrs. Burns, we got a lot of pictures like this one, and we got a lot of others from the computer, on Web sites."*

"Good, Francisco, I see you have quite a few here. I have a couple more books at home on rain forests that I can bring in for you to use. I'll bring them in tomorrow. Students in the other groups are finding good photographs too. You can use the photos to go along with your writing in your report."

"James, what about you?"

"Mrs. Burns, I been finding rain forests on the map in this geography book, see, but I suck at reading maps, so I only found just one of them; it's in Africa."

"Well, James, if map reading is hard for you, why don't you just switch with someone in your group and work on something else, like writing down descriptions of the rain forest. You're much better at writing, so just do that, OK? At least you tried! I'll find you a good book that describes the rain forest. Then you can write up some descriptions for the report. I'll bet you can get an A for your part in writing the description."

Mrs. Burns moves to another group, asks playfully, "OK, guys, let's see your work."

In many ways, this is a typical fifth-grade science curricula, and these are typical school activities. Students collaborate on topics, the reports for which eventually become whole-class presentations. Mrs. Burns sets the assignment, determines the study guide questions, and grades the final projects. She conducts formative assessment to monitor progress, and students are held accountable for their accomplishment. Let us put aside the actual classroom activities for now and, instead, pay close attention to the *language* of the classroom. Just as linguists distinguish between the surface structure of language (the actual words) and the deep structure (concepts), so too does the language of classroom exchanges reveal deep meanings about learning and learners, responsibility and effort, intelligence and enterprise, and so too does this language help to build profound beliefs about engaging learners *as capable learners*.

Mrs. Burns seems to be thoughtful about word choices. She reinforces Andrea's wise academic decisions ("Good to list them all like that"). With Francisco, she rewards productivity ("Good, Francisco, I see you have quite a few here"). For James, she spares him the frustrations of map reading and steers him instead toward his strength ("You're much better at writing, so just do that"). But in spite of her desire to support her students' efforts, she innocently misses opportunities to support their efforts as learners. For example, she gives James false praise for effort ("At least you tried!"), and when she offers to find resources for Francisco ("I have a couple more books at home on rain forests that I can bring in for you to use"), she inadvertently suggests that he may not be able to find more materials himself.

Brains exist in order to learn; they cannot *not* learn, unless they are prevented from doing so, such as by a brain injury. Those synapses are always firing, and students' brains are always paying attention to the way teachers talk about them. As you shall see below, if we choose words to describe our students as agents of their own learning, they are more likely to become active seekers of knowledge as their brains work to construct and refine learning *naturally*. How we talk about students as learners contributes to how those students willingly and comfortably accept learning challenges.

Students thrive when the discourse of the classroom encourages them to become mindful of themselves as learners and when they are supported in their efforts to become attuned to themselves as learners. As you will see, when students view intelligence as something they can get better at rather than something that is unchanging, they become smarter and their achievement improves. In this chapter, therefore, we look more closely at the exchanges of talk between teachers and students in order to understand how talk can function in classrooms to build and support genuine engagement. To get to this understanding, let us consider two lines of inquiry about classroom talk: first, talking about learning; second, talking about intelligence.

TALKING ABOUT LEARNING

In *Choice Words: How Our Language Affects Children's Learning*, Peter H. Johnston (2004*) shows how "those things teachers say (and don't say) . . . changes the literate lives of students" (p. 2) by helping them become independent and engaged learners. Our words, Johnston says, impact student achievement in both positive and negative ways. "Language has 'content,'" he says, "but it also bears information about the speaker and how he or she views the listener and their assumed relationship" (p. 6).

For instance, when Mrs. Burns volunteers to bring in a book from home for Francisco, her supportive gesture (on the surface, it is a kind offer) to help him in his search for information denies him *agency*—that is, it relieves him of his responsibility to find books that *he* believes are important; indeed, *she* determines that he needs more books ("I have a couple more books at home on rain forests for you to use"), that she knows what books he needs in particular, and that she, not *he*, knows where to find them. Her heart may be in the right place, but her actual words run the risk of making him think he's not capable or independent enough to find books on his subject himself. It is a subtle message that says, "You are the kind of person who cannot figure out things for yourself" (Johnston, 2004, p. 8).

Along with many linguists, Johnston (2004) says that classroom language "creates realities and identities." For example, the "implications of talking about reading as 'work' are different from referring to it as 'fun.' Similarly, telling children they can have free choice time, 'but first we have to finish our reading,' positions reading poorly simply by using the words 'have to'" (p. 9). The words of instructional conversations between teachers and students affect how students think about their intellectual powers as well as their affective powers. When we really think about classroom talk, we become more deliberate in choosing the words of engagement. Let us look at some categories of the language of engagement Johnston identifies.

Noticing and Naming

We recognize patterns in our experiences, and from these patterns we form beliefs, conceptions, and neural representations in our brains. Were we not to rely on pattern recognition, the world would be pure chaos to us; it would be non-sense, meaning-*less*. Meaning-*full*, natural learning invites students to notice and name what connects. Our language ought to reflect our faith in their ability to make those connections. We can invite students to notice and name by saying things such as the following:

- "Who notices . . . (e.g., how animals develop parts of their bodies in response to the challenges of their environment)?"
- "Did anyone notice anything that surprised you in your reading?"
- "Did you discover anything else that was like this?"

Identity

"Building an identity means coming to see in ourselves the characteristics of particular categories (and roles) of people and developing a sense of what it feels like to be that sort of person and belong in certain social spaces" writes Johnston (2004, p. 23). Learners are always trying on different identities. "When I grow up, I want to be a . . ." they say. Likewise, the ways in which we talk with them in classroom interactions can often contribute positively to experimental or emerging identities:

- "Scientists just like you believe the same thing about evolution."
- "As a writer, what other ways can you think of to say this?"
- "I wonder if you could find another reader in this room who would agree with you about your interpretation."

Building identities through our talk helps students see themselves as character types "in the storylines in which they emplot themselves," Johnston (2004) notes. "Teachers' comments can offer them, and nudge them toward, productive identities" (p. 23).

Agency

If we'd like students to believe that they can act on their own behalf, solve problems in school, take action to reach goals, and become strategic, then our talk with them must reflect that wish. Our conversations with students, Johnston (2004) says, "show how, by acting strategically, they accomplish things, and at the same time, that they are the kind of person who accomplishes things" (p. 30). Agency language notices and acknowledges students' actions:

- "How did you figure that one out?"
- "How are you planning to solve that problem?"
- "What will you do next?"
- "That's interesting. Why do you think . . . ?"

Instilling a sense of agency through our words has direct bearing on students' learning. Johnston (2004) notes that students "who doubt their competence set low goals and choose easy tasks, and they plan poorly. When they face difficulties, they become confused, lose concentration, and start telling themselves stories about their own incompetence. In the long run, they disengage, decrease effort, generate fewer ideas, and become passive and discouraged" (p. 40).

Generalizing

Learners generalize when they transfer learning from one thing to another—for example, from a past or current experience to a future one or from something familiar to the unfamiliar. When they transfer learning strategies, in particular, they are more likely to understand that some strategies may succeed while others may not. We don't want learners to say, "Well, that didn't work. Guess I don't know what to do now!" Instead, we want them to say, "Well, that didn't work. I wonder if this other way might be better?" Our classroom language can support generalizing abilities:

- "What is another way you might approach this math problem?"
- "You had this problem in the last story you wrote. Do you remember how you approached it then?"
- "When you read about the rainforests in Africa, did that remind you at all of the ones in South America? How so?"
- "What if you . . . ?"

What-if talk can be especially important in nurturing imaginative "mind experiments" that "allow us to notice things that are otherwise too naturalized to be noticed, and help us use our experience to understand possible events we have not experienced" (Johnston, 2004, p. 48).

Knowing

Knowing means that knowledge is legitimately generated and passed on *by learners* as well as by teachers, as opposed to knowledge that is only possessed and transmitted by teachers *to students*. How we talk with students about the origins and transmission of knowledge says something epistemologically about who has an active role in constructing knowledge (teachers and/or students) as well as who has ownership over knowledge:

- "Hmm. Let me say that back to you to see if I've got it right. I really want to be sure I understand you."
- "Wow. I never would have thought of it that way; that is very interesting."
- "How did you come to that conclusion?"

Knowledge-validating language sends a message that the speaker's ideas are not only memorable but also can be a foundation upon which other knowledge can build.

Democratic Learning Community

Johnston (2004) reminds us that genuinely engaging classrooms are more likely to come about when they are democratic learning communities where "students grow into the intellectual life around them." Such classrooms enable learners to risk "trying out new strategies and concepts and stretching themselves intellectually" (p. 65). The language of such classrooms encourages learners to exercise intellectual respect and empathy as they appreciate difference and explore alternity:

- "Are there any other ways to think about that?"
- "You and your table figured that out by yourselves. How did you do that?"
- "I wonder how she feels about that?"

I-wonder language is particularly important in building democratic learning communities because it offers possibility, tentative exploration, and hypothetical ideas as invitations to think or feel differently. Such hypothetical language, while not "valued in school accountability systems, is very highly valued in the professional world" (Johnston, 2004,

p. 69). This exploratory talk "brings multiple minds together to work on the same problem in the most powerful ways" (p. 68).

Teacher language, as Johnston's (2004) research makes clear, has the power to shape students' identities as learners and help them understand how their brains and their hearts work in tandem to improve achievement. Talking about learning in these ways dives below the surface of learning—to those places where agency and identity exist in formative ways.

TALKING ABOUT INTELLIGENCE

The words we use to help students become engaged have a subtext running through them that implies a view of *intelligence.* That is to say, *how* students—and we—talk about intelligence can affect students' motivation and performance in school and elsewhere. Carol S. Dweck's research (2002*, 2006) shows how people's *beliefs* about their intelligence affects their school behavior and consequently their motivation and achievement. Students hold theories about their own intelligence, and those theories are most often tacit: Students aren't even aware of which view they believe in, but their behaviors and how they describe their behaviors give insight into their tacit beliefs; and beliefs drive their behaviors. As Dweck (2002) notes, students "with the right beliefs and the right commitment" (p.39) amaze us with what they can accomplish. So why, she asks, "do some very bright students do poorly in school and end up achieving little in life" while other "seemingly less bright students rise to the challenges and accomplish far more than anyone ever expected?" (p. 37).

In answering this question, Dweck (2002) describes two views of intelligence that are key components of students' eagerness to learn, their love of challenge, and their ability to persist and thrive in the face of difficulty. "This is why they are key factors in what students achieve" (p. 37).

Fixed Intelligence

If you believe that your intelligence is a fixed trait, then you can do little to change it, but you can also do a lot to disguise your "lack of intelligence" to save face. After all, you think, you only have just so much intelligence, or just some kind of intelligence, and that's it—and it cannot be developed because it's fixed. Students who believe their intelligence is fixed want to look smart. Since they only have a certain amount of it or a certain kind, they want to protect what they have, especially if what they have is threatened by a task that they perceive to be too challenging. Given a choice between a task that challenges them and one that they know they can do well, they choose the latter—because it is *safer* and will make them look smart.

For those who hold the fixed view, failure indicates something lacking in their intellectual ability. They believe that working harder is worthless because either you have it or you don't. Period. In Dweck's (2002) view, "There is no more damaging view for students than the belief that effort is unnecessary (if you're smart) and ineffective (if you're not). And it goes right along with a view of intelligence." Thus, fixed-intelligence students "are prone to a variety of self-defeating behaviors" (p. 43), such as leaving things to the last minute, giving up when the going gets tough, losing interest suddenly, or blaming others for their inability to excel.

Malleable Intelligence

If you believe intelligence is a malleable trait, you believe it is capable of developing—with the right strategy, or more time, or a different approach, and so on. You think that hard work really does pay off, that grades don't accurately measure true abilities, and that learning involves risks worth taking, regardless of how you may appear to others. You would agree that "it is much more important in my classes to learn things than it is to get the best grades" or "I like school work I can learn from even if I make a lot of mistakes." Failure "sends a message about your effort or strategy, not your fixed ability. Mistakes are simply a natural part of learning, and give you information about what to do next" (Dweck, 2002, p. 44). The secret to success lies in finding the right strategy, working harder, or working differently, for effort truly does make a difference. For those with the malleable view, difficulty means only that you have to work more on something or you have to approach the task in another way that may hold more promise—and you aren't afraid to try because even if you do fail, it only means that your strategy wasn't right, not that you weren't smart enough.

Talking About Intelligence

Both views of intelligence have some validity (i.e., some people may well inherit genetic "natural" abilities, while some may do well because they are so passionate about succeeding). The danger of the fixed view is its potential to discredit and distort genuine accomplishment through hard, strategic work. Dweck (2002) recommends that we attend to the ways in which we talk with students in order to orient them away from fixed views and toward malleable views instead.

Intelligence Praise

The main way that we can promote malleable views is through praise that focuses on effort, not intelligence. For example, when students do well at a task, we can say, "Wow. You did really well. You must be smart at this problem" (fixed view) or we can say, "Wow. You did really well. You must have worked hard at this problem" (malleable view). Instead of making comments that reflect a fixed intellectual trait, as in "You just don't have a knack for reading informational texts; why don't you stick to narrative?" we can say, "How did you read this article? I wonder if you tried to write ten-word summaries along the way, would that be a better strategy for you? I know you can read it; you just need another way of understanding it." Asking "What did you learn?" (malleable) versus "What grade did you get?" (fixed) is yet another way of praising the effort inherent in malleable intelligence.

In Dweck's (2002) research, "The different forms of intelligence praise had a clear impact on students' theories of intelligence." While fixed-intelligence-praised students rejected tasks that did not make them look smart, effort-praised students were "eager to jump right in and learn" (p. 48). Indeed, effort-praised students enjoyed learning more, and they were more engaged and challenged by difficulty. In contrast, if the fixed-intelligence students did not do well on a task, "they could not enjoy it as much" (p. 49).

So what can we do to promote the malleable view of intelligence in order to create, through classroom talk, more engaged learning?

- Demystify intelligence. Talk with students about the different views. Cite examples of "smart" people, such as Michael Jordan or Michelle Obama, and note how practice contributed to Jordan's extraordinary "talent" or how hard academic work paid off for Obama.
- Avoid giving trait-focused feedback. "Do not praise children for low challenge, low effort, no-mistake success. . . . This will not make them love learning and challenge" (Dweck, 2002, p. 54).
- Give effort praise that highlights *processes*—"You must have really worked hard"—and praise *strategies:* "You found a great way to solve that problem" (Dweck, 2002, p. 51).
- Become a spokesperson for the malleable trait values you want your students to take on. I know teachers who say to students, "Hmm. Now *that's* a good problem" and "I just love being confused like this!" and "Well, that one didn't work, so let's see what else we can do instead."
- Show students how to be successful; give direct instruction in alternative strategies—and model those strategies.
- Balance good grades with good learning. We might say, for example, "Are you proud of the grade you earned? Why?" Or "I know you worked really hard on that project. What does your grade on it say about what you learned or how you improved?"

- Adopt belief-altering language—speak about "challenges as won-derful opportunities" and "mistakes as though they are fascinating and helpful friends" (Dweck, 2002, p. 58).

SCIENCE CLASS REVISITED

How we talk about students' learning and intelligence sends implicit messages about who they are as learners and about how they might become better, more successful—and more engaged—learners. Unless we are thoughtful and deliberate in how we talk about learning and how we talk about intelligence, we risk devaluing students' worth as learners as well as their prospects for achievement. To create the optimal conditions for flow in our classrooms, we need to use the language of flow that is most likely to engage.

The words Mrs. Burns chooses to talk about learning and intelligence can inform her decisions about engagement:

- *Mind:* Words can reinforce students' natural ways of *noticing pat-terns* in their learning and acknowledge their natural abilities to *generalize learning strategies* to other situations. Students' percep-tions about their minds' capabilities will be shaped by how Mrs. Burns talks with them about fixed and malleable intelligence.
- *Heart:* Words can help to counteract learned helplessness and prove to students that they can succeed by instilling a sense of agency and forming identities as successful protagonists in the stories they tell about themselves as well as in the ways they think about their intelligence.
- *Flow:* How we describe learning tasks has the power to suggest that learning is enjoyable, that challenge can be engaging, that work can also be pleasure, and that success comes with effort and alter-native strategies.

Let us return to Mrs. Burns' classroom and see how she might revise how she talks about learning and intelligence. Can you tell how the fol-lowing alternative ways of talking get at more supportive views of learn-ing and intelligence?

- **Before**: *"So how is your work coming on the three parts of the study guide? Which one are you on, Andrea?"*
- **After:** *"So Andrea, what are you noticing about the rain forests? Where are you in your research?"*

- **Before**: *Andrea flips to her assignment worksheet, her finger poised in the middle of the page. "Well," she begins, "we sorta skipped the first one about describing the rain forest and went to the second one about the animals and plants that live there 'cause that was more interesting and we started listing all the animals there—monkeys, jaguars, snakes, um, we have them on our list here!"*

   "That's good," says Mrs. Burns. "Good to list them all like that. But you have a long way to go because there are a lot more animals in the rain forest than just those three. Not that you have to have all of them down, but three is hardly a start."

- **After:** *"That was smart of you to start with what interests you the most and then come back to the other parts. Are you noticing anything about the types of animals there and the environment itself?*

   _____

- **Before**: *"What other work have you done? Francisco?"*
- **After:** *"How is your research coming along, Francisco? What are you learning?"*

   _____

- **Before:** *Francisco opens April Pulley Sayre's book* Tropical Rain Forests *and shows his teacher a picture. "See, Mrs. Burns, we got a lot of pictures like this one, and we got a lot of others from the computer, on Web sites."*

   "Good, Francisco, I see you have quite a few here. I have a couple more books at home on rain forests that I can bring in for you to use. I'll bring them in tomorrow. Students in the other groups are finding good photographs too."

- **After:** *"Wow. You have some really interesting photos here, Francisco. Are you satisfied with the ones you have or do you know where to find more? Researchers in the other groups are finding good photographs too."*

   _____

- **Before:** *"You can use the photos to go along with your writing in your report."*
- **After**: *"I wonder how you'll use the photos to go along with the writing in your research report. What are your thoughts on how you'll do that?"*

   _____

- **Before**: *"James, what about you?"*
- **After**: *"James, you look like you are working with the geography of the rain forest. What are you finding that's interesting?"*

   _____

- **Before:** *"Mrs. Burns, I been finding rain forests on the map in this geography book, see, but I suck at reading maps, so I only found just one of them; it's in Africa."*

   "Well, James, if map reading is hard for you, why don't you just switch with someone in your group and work on something else, like writing down descriptions of the rain forest. You're a much better student at writing, so just do that, OK?"

- **After:** *"I understand you that you think map reading is hard, so can you tell me how you go about reading maps?*

Or

- **After:** *"So that's one way of reading maps, but there are others. I wonder what would happen if you tried another strategy? Here, let me show you another way to read maps. See this part here? It's called a legend. I'm going to read the legend before I read the map and see if that might help me make more sense out of the map. How about if I start and then you help out?"*

How we talk with students about themselves as learners and about their intelligence affects not only what they think and feel about themselves but also how willing they are to become engaged in learning. Having a fellow teacher or friend observe our teaching, and audio- or videotaping ourselves talking with students, would give us much insight into the dynamics of discourse in our classrooms.

Changing our talking ways is not simple. If it were just a matter of finding the right words to say to students, we could just memorize a few choice words or phrases, and that would be that, you might be thinking. But there is much more to engaged learning when it comes to classroom discourse. In the next chapter, we extend our look at talk in the classroom by examining what happens when we promote engaged learning through discussion.

Using Discussions to Engage Learners

Most of the Biology 1 students have done the assigned reading on the structure of the cell, but when their teacher invites them to discuss the reading, here's how it goes:

Mr. Mason begins with, "OK, so what do we know about the cell? How big is it?

"Tiny." says Christine. "Very tiny."

"How tiny? Can you see it with the naked eye or do you need a microscope?"

"Microscope."

"Good, Christine. Now, how many parts does the cell have, four, five, six? Anyone? Gerald?

"Don't remember, Mr. Mason, four?"

"No, three."

"Oh, sorry."

"That's OK. C'mon, people, you did the reading, didn't you? Who can tell me what these three parts are?

The students uniformly begin thumbing through the pages of the text, looking for the answer. Slowly, Raul raises his hand. "Here it is, one part is the membrane."

"Good, Raul, keep going."

"And another is the, uh, cy-to-plas-im. And the third one is the DNA part, right, the DNA."

"Excellent. So then, what does it mean if I say that cells are monophyletic? Here, I'll write that word on the board. Who knows what that means?"

More thumbing through the pages; some students go to the glossary in the back of the book to look up the word. Mr. Mason waits patiently. Finally, Shelly reads from the glossary definition: "Of or concerning a single phylum of plants or animals." She looks up from her book, a puzzled expression on her face.

"Yes, Shelly, and that means that cells are all descended from a single founder cell. In other words, all the cells on Earth come from one starter cell and all have the same basic structure or shared features. And that is why it is considered by biologists to be the universal unit of life."

The discussion continues along these lines, with Mr. Mason asking direct questions designed to elicit specific answers, the students either sheepishly searching for the answers right on the page, or outright guessing. Mr. Mason, to his credit, waits for them while they do the hard work of finding answers. Many of us wouldn't wait, but would, instead, supply the answer in hurried attempts to "cover the material." Although Mr. Mason calls the exchange a "discussion," it is really a recitation. As a recitation, it has its proper place in classrooms—usually to check on understanding of specific facts or procedures or to be sure that students have achieved a very basic level of reading comprehension, generally at the literal level. The form of this recitation seems familiar too, as it is popularly known as IRE, where teacher *initiates*, students *respond*, and teacher *evaluates* students' response (Mehan, 1979).

Unfortunately, this IRE pattern is the most prevalent form of teacher–student exchange in American classrooms, with teachers standing in front of students and working hard to elicit talk that would ideally become an engaging discussion of subjects but most often remains where it begins—a teacher-centered interrogation. One reason so many students find school boring or unengaging is that what is supposed to pass for classroom discussion is more often yet one more take on IRE recitation.

Engaged discussion also has its place in the classroom, though it is more rare. Think back to any lively, substantive classroom discussion in which you were thoroughly involved. What do you recall about it? That there was some respect shown for your ideas? That your fellow discussants actually listened to you and vice versa? That you had opportunity to direct the discussion at times? That what you talked about really mattered to you personally, emotionally, or cognitively? That you felt safe? I'm sure most, if not all, of these qualities were present, but how did they come to be? Was it just happenstance that the discussion engaged you? Or could it be that the teacher orchestrated the class to create optimal conditions for the flow of engaging discussion? Or was it a combination of luck and artful teaching?

Let us try to answer these questions by examining key dimensions of discussion aimed at flow. It is impossible to discuss here all the possible components of engaged discussion, for that would take volumes. It is possible, however, to focus on key components that reflect brain-based research as well as humanistic principles of engaged learning—and that are borne out by research on engaging discussions.

ENGAGING IDEAS

Recall again a time when you were involved in a genuine discussion that mattered. What made it matter? Was it that you wanted to learn more? That you wanted to teach something? Were you emotionally involved in the outcome of the discussion? Were you personally connected to the topic? Did something someone said pique your interest? Were you invited to challenge another's ideas or defend your own? Did you face a dilemma and see the discussion as a way of resolving the dilemma? Was the topic close to your values, or did it challenge your values? Was it a question posed in such a way that you had to make a decision among apparently equal possibilities?

Any one of these reasons or any combination of them and others may account for your engagement in the discussion. What made it a "discussion" was the give and take of human discourse about ideas that seemed important at the time. In good classroom discussions, teachers find ways to start with statements or questions that could have been taken right off the World Question Center Web site (www.edge.org), questions such as "What is the most important word in this story?" "Why should this historical information be hidden from children?" or "Why is this scientific discovery dangerous?" Some teachers kick things off with experiments or other physical events involving artifacts of some sort, such as the English teacher who begins a discussion of Hawthorne's "The Birthmark" with a bright crimson mark on her cheek. Some teachers hook students by challenging authority, like the poetry teacher who loves to begin the discussion of a poem this way: "Everybody thinks Frost's poem is about making one choice over another, but is that really what it's about?" Some teachers draw students in by challenging imagination, as in the case of the math teacher who stands before the class and says, "OK, that was the most common way to solve this problem, but there is another way, one that will make you a math genius if you can figure it out. Who has some ideas on what that way could be?" Other teachers set up mind hypotheses: A music teacher says, "What do you think would happen if we added a B flat in a few places?"

Engaged discussion depends, first, on engaging ideas. The problem with poor or boring class discussions is that too often they miss this crucial point. They don't begin with what is most engaging, the stuff that piques curiosity. Teacher and researcher John Barell (2003) wonders what is worth talking about in classrooms where the onus is on teachers to cover the curriculum. His answer is that we should look for the "big ideas" in our subject areas, those concepts that challenge students to think. Some would call these "essential questions," but the idea is the same. Barell lists some of the big ideas by content areas and I abbreviate them here:

- History and social studies: The development, change, and decay of societies and political and economic systems
- Mathematics: Equalities, limits, patterns, symmetry, congruency
- Life sciences: The nature of living things, ecosystems, the cell, DNA
- Physical sciences: Cause-and-effect relationships and pressure, force, and motion
- Earth sciences: The solar system, stars and galaxies, Earth
- The arts: Elements of composition: line, texture, light, balance, and so on; the creation of symbols and representations of reality
- Foreign languages: Structure and syntax of language, culture, the nature of dialects
- Technology: New technologies; problem solving in everyday life
- Physical education: Physical fitness, wellness, games, play (pp. 73–75)

Barell (2003) would have discussions that challenge students to think about big ideas such as these. Further, he would have discussions that illuminate "the intellectual processes that people in these disciplines use to acquire new knowledge" (p. 75), as I tried to point out in the chapter on modeling.

Another way of getting at subjects that matter is to discuss ideas that are value laden and that speak to the values held by students, such as these:

- Is _____ right?
- Is _____ fair?
- Is _____ (right/wrong/just) to _____?
- What is the most important _____ (word, sentence, graph) in this story, poem, essay, experiment, problem, and so on?
- Why do you think some people believe _____ about _____?
- What does someone have to believe in order to (agree/disagree) that _____?

Such question stems as these easily adapt to any subject area. For instance, in government class, a teacher starts off a discussion of voting rights with, "Is it right to allow people with serious mental illnesses to vote?" In world history, a teacher shows a map of Africa in the early twentieth century and asks, "What problems do you think might be created when tribal boundaries differ from country boundaries, such as what we see on this map?"

Engaged discussion begins with engaging ideas. That takes thoughtful planning as we query our subjects for the big ideas that are there. It demands careful attention to the language we use to introduce engaging ideas, as I tried to emphasize in the example, where value-laden words are deliberately chosen in advance. Finally, it takes a good understanding of questions, as we will see next.

ENGAGING QUESTIONS

"Teachers spend between anywhere from thirty-five to fifty percent of their instructional time conducting questioning sessions . . . and the questions they ask have potential for increasing students' classroom participation and achievement" (Cotton, 1988*, p. 1). Many teachers distinguish between *authentic* and *inauthentic* questions, the former being those with no predetermined answer while the latter are those for which teachers already know the answer. Mehan (1979) shows the difference in this way:

Authentic Question:

1. Speaker A: What time is it, Denise?

2. Speaker B: 2:30

3. Speaker A: Thank you, Denise.

Inauthentic Question:

1. Speaker A: What time is it, Denise?

2. Speaker B: 2:30

3. Speaker A: Very good, Denise.

In the IRE format (initiation-response-evaluation), inauthentic questions predominate because the function of the format is to elicit brief, known-to-the-teacher bits of information, such as when we check on reading comprehension ("Who is the main character in this story?") or classroom procedures ("Is this something we write in our class planner?").

Both inauthentic and authentic questions have their place in classrooms because they elicit different needed responses. Typically, more inauthentic questions are asked than authentic questions, and authentic questions more strongly influence engagement in classroom discussion. It is helpful to think of what we want our questions to *do*, what we expect the questions to generate as student response. Question researchers Morgan and Saxton (1992) suggest that "whatever the question you ask, whatever its kind and function, the first guide in asking questions is think about *how the question will help students engage in (feeling) and with (thought) the material*" (p. 72, italics in original).

Morgan and Saxton (1992) classify questions according to how they function (that is, what teachers want the question to do). The following categories and examples are drawn from Chapter 5 of their book.

Category A: Questions that elicit information. These are the questions that draw out what is already known in terms of both information and experience and which establish the appropriate procedures for conducting the work. Examples include the following:

- Questions that establish procedure, as in, "How much time do you need?"
- Questions that focus on recall of facts, as in, "What is the formula?"
- Questions that unify the class, as in, "Are we ready to go on?"

Category B: Questions that shape understanding. These are questions that help teachers and students fill in what lies between the facts and sort out, express, and elaborate upon how they are thinking and feeling about the material. Examples include the following:

- Questions that focus on making connections, as in, "What connections are there between this and the kinds of things that happen in our own lives?"
- Questions that demand inference and interpretation, as in, "What might be implied by this sentence?"
- Questions that focus on meanings that lie behind the actual content, as in, "What is this case really about?"

Category C: Questions that press for reflection. These are the questions that demand intellectual and emotional commitment by challenging the individual to think critically and creatively. Examples include the following:

- Questions that develop supposition or hypothesis, as in, "Suppose the man is discovered to be a veterinarian—what then?"
- Questions that focus on personal feelings, as in, "What was in your mind when you read this passage?"

- Questions that focus on future action/projection, as in, "What are the consequences for the three who are left?"
- Questions that develop critical assessments/value judgments, as in, "How can we justify the amount of material we hurl into outer space?"

While it is easy to see that Category A questions are more likely to be of the inauthentic variety, whereas questions in Categories B and C generate more authentic, higher-order responses, Morgan and Saxton (1992) remind us that these categories are not hierarchical: Inauthentic questions are not "bad" any more than authentic questions are "good." They are simply different, and they serve different purposes. For example, reading teachers use Category A questions to elicit "right there" responses, as in "The answer is right there in the text." They use Category B and C questions when students need to read between the lines, draw from different parts of the text, or go beyond the text to make connections with their personal experiences, speculate on the unknown, or create hypotheses.

Thoughtful teachers will ask questions from each category depending on what they want the questions to do. What is crucial, however, is that we not expect inauthentic questions to generate discussion because, by their very form, they don't elicit responses that shape understanding or press for reflection. That's why questions that partake of Category B and C qualities may be considered authentic questions that have the potential to generate discussions. All other things being equal, better questions generate better discussions. So does silence.

ENGAGING SILENCE

Although it seems counterintuitive, silence can go a long way toward sustaining engaged discussion. We all know those moments of passionate outburst in discussions when students just can't wait to join in, when their enthusiasm cannot be contained. I love those moments and certainly do not want to quash them. But moments of deliberate silence also have a generative effect on discussion, especially when we use silence judiciously to promote robust thinking and feeling.

Most of us are familiar with the term *wait time*, those seconds that elapse between when we ask a question and when the first student responds. Wait-time researcher Mary Budd Rowe (1986*) calls this time juncture "Wait Time 1" and distinguishes it from "Wait Time 2," which is the time that elapses between the student's response and our response to the student. Rowe found that both wait times seldom take more than 1.5 seconds and are typically less than a second (0.9 seconds). In the familiar IRE model (see the beginning of this chapter), teachers ask many questions quickly, take brief answers quickly, and then move on to the next question, beginning their reactions to students or asking the next question immediately. When teachers extended both Wait Time 1 and Wait Time 2 to at least three seconds, however, Rowe found significant positive effects on student talk and student thinking:

- The length of student responses increased between 300% and 700%, in some cases more.
- More inferences were supported by evidence and logical argument.
- Speculative thinking increased.
- The number of questions asked by students increased, and (in science classes) the number of experiments they proposed increased.
- Student–student exchanges increased; teacher-centered "show and tell" behavior decreased.
- Failure to respond decreased.
- Disciplinary moves decreased.
- The variety of students participating voluntarily in discussion increased, and the number of unsolicited, but appropriate, contributions by students increased.
- Student confidence, as reflected in fewer inflectional responses, increased.
- Achievement improved on written measures where the items are cognitively complex.

Interestingly, Rowe (1986*) also found that increasing both wait times has positive effects on teachers:

- Teachers' responses exhibited greater flexibility, as indicated by the occurrence of fewer discourse errors and greater continuity in the development of ideas.
- Teachers asked more questions asking for clarification or inviting elaboration or contrary positions.
- Teachers' expectations for typically quiet students changed as "invisible students" became more visible in discussions with longer wait times, an effect Rowe found to be particularly pronounced for minority students.

Unmistakably, longer durations for Wait Time 1 and Wait Time 2 add generative and reflective qualities to discussion, for they encourage among students and teachers alike the thoughtful habits of mind associated with engaged learning—elaborating, clarifying, and revising ideas;

as well as speculating, reasoning, and supporting claims with evidence. When coupled with engaging ideas and engaging questions, silence has a profound effect on promoting discussion. Let us now look in some detail at the dynamics of discussion.

THE DYNAMICS OF ENGAGING DISCUSSION

We work hard to have lively and engaging discussion in our classrooms. Some of the time we succeed, some of the time we do not. We know when discussion is a problem, but we don't always know why or what we can do about it. Even when students are onto engaging subjects, even when we pose deep questions, and, yes, even when wait time is naturally integrated into class time, things just don't always go as well as they should. Why not?

Much insight into the dynamics of discussion may be found in the research results of a team led by Martin Nystrand (Nystrand & Gamoran, 1991*; Nystrand, Gamoran, Kachur, & Pendergast, 1997*; Nystrand, Wu, Gamoran, Zeiser, & Long, 2003*). Just as IRE Category A questions put teachers at center stage until they pose Category B and C questions that turn the discussion into a student-centered one, so too can discussions shift from teacher-centered (*monologic*) to teacher/student-centered (*dialogic*). In monologic classroom discourse, teachers' voices dominate as they ask questions with known answers (inauthentic), focus on establishing literal levels of understanding ("The answer is right there in the text"), validate the correctness of student responses ("Good!"), and maintain a hierarchy of authority whereby teachers ask and students answer. As stated above, such discourse is important in checking reading comprehension, establishing common names and terms, and reviewing classroom management procedures as well as basic content (e.g., "What do we call a _____?").

By contrast, in dialogic discourse, students share center stage as teachers ask Category B and C questions, validate students' responses in a variety of ways that recognize the content of students' responses (e.g., "Good point! It's an awful way to lose trust!"), and encourage students to elaborate and clarify their thoughts and ideas (e.g., "That's interesting! Why do you feel that way about this issue?"). Teachers use dialogic discourse to prime cognitive and affective pumps, engender imaginative and speculative journeys, and help students who are struggling to construct meaning as they think and speak.

Based on data collected in effective classroom discussions, Nystrand and colleagues (2003) looked for those episodes in a class discussion where discourse shifted from monologic to dialogic and back again, and then they analyzed each episode to understand how the dynamics changed each time. They discovered that when dialogic discussions occur, student engagement increases, along with student academic achievement. These researchers found five indicators that contribute positively to the dynamics of engaged dialogic discussion.

Authentic questions. As stated earlier in this chapter, authentic questions have no predetermined answers. When we ask mostly authentic questions, students learn that what they say really does matter in the discussion, as Nystrand et al. (2003) point out: "Authentic questions posed by the teacher signal to students that the teacher is interested in what they think and know . . . open the floor to students' ideas . . . [and] invite students to contribute something new to the class interaction" (pp. 144–145).

Uptake. We ask a question and a student responds. Then we use what that student has said in our response and in follow-up instruction. We "take up" from the student's comment and do something with it; *using their own words*, we validate by repeating it or paraphrasing it: "Uptake is important because it recognizes and envelops the importance of the student contribution" (Nystrand et al., 2003, p. 146). Here are some examples:

- "So, are you saying that _____?"
- "Let me say this back to you to be sure I understand you."
- "Is that anything like what Josh just said about _____?"
- "If it's true what you say about _____, then is it also true that _____?"

Level of evaluation. In the IRE model, we typically evaluate student responses with short comments such as "Good" and "Right." In dialogic discussion, however, such abbreviated evaluations are coupled with substantive comments that elaborate upon students' remarks, such as the following:

- "Good point; this really *is* a dilemma."
- "That's an interesting way of thinking about it; your comment reminds me of _____."
- "I like the way you talk about that part of the equation because _____."

The effect of evaluating in this way is that by restating what students say, we validate their comments, in effect saying that what they said is important enough to remember it, link it to other knowledge, or let them know that we appreciate learning from them.

Cognitive level of questions. Lower cognitive levels include recitation and factual recall; higher levels include hypothesizing, speculation, and analysis. Generally, the higher the cognitive challenge, the more likely it is that students will be engaged. But we must be aware that cognitive challenge is both context- and student-specific and depends on a number of factors alone and in combination:

- *Knowledgeability of the person answering the question.* For example, if Student A doesn't know quite how to respond to a question but Student B does and only needs to recite the answer, then Student A faces the real cognitive challenge.
- *Experience, ability, and prior knowledge of the person answering the question.* If Student A seldom wrestles with hypothetical questions but Student B has much experience thinking through them, then Student A will be more challenged cognitively.
- *Nature of the instructional activity.* Chapter review questions, for instance, that ask for applications to contexts not previously considered will elicit higher-order thinking more so than will factual recall questions.
- *Source of information required by the question.* Cognitive level is influenced by where students must find information to respond to questions. Recall from a lecture, reading from notes, or pointing to a passage in a text require low-level cognitive challenge, whereas application to contexts beyond the text or analyzing parallel situations elsewhere call for more cognitive challenge.

Question source. Students' questions are uniformly authentic: They "don't ask questions when they already know the answer" (Nystrand et al., 2003, p. 188). Student questions are the most important contributor to dialogic discussion. Although I have focused much attention here on the cognitive challenge of *our* questions, it is student questions that ignite the most engaging classroom discussions. We all know the experience of a student asking just the right question at just the right time in such a way that it energizes and animates class discussion. On the flip side, we also know the danger of student questions that derail discussion or offend others. But the insight here is to be on the lookout for student questions that work, to seize the moment, and then to build instruction around those questions.

From this research, what do we know about the dynamics of discussion? One, we know that authentic, higher-order teacher questions are more likely to create, guide, and sustain the momentum of discussion.

Two, when we treat students as legitimate sources of knowledge and opinion, we validate their minds and spirits such that they know they are being invited into a genuine community of learners. Three, getting to engaging discussion is hard work, and it is more complex than we may have thought. I like the metaphor Nystrand et al. (2003) use in their research to describe the process of moving a class toward quality discussion: "Getting a discussion going is a little like building a fire: With enough kindling of the right sort, accompanied by patience, and along with the spark of student engagement, ignition is possible" (p. 190). That is our goal—passionate, indeed fiery, discussions.

BIOLOGY 1 REVISITED

When Mr. Mason plans his cell structure lesson this time, he tries to predict students' engagement in discussion:

- *Mind*: Engaging ideas involve students in meaningful searches for understanding; students can encounter the very tensions characteristic of flow experiences, and cognitive dissonance can move them deeper into learning.
- *Heart*: Students are socially involved with one another, often making value decisions, and always feeling personally valued and their questions intellectually valued. They have opportunity to make deeper connections with their own values, ethics, and beliefs as well as to encounter others' ways of thinking about these matters.
- *Flow*: What discussion affords in terms of flow states is immediate feedback, both feedback-in-action and feedback-after-action; it also affords opportunity for students to enjoy discussion for its own sake.

Instead of beginning the class with a review of the basic facts of cell structure, Mr. Mason might begin with an engaging idea, some thought that invites students to make a decision about the cell. For instance, *New York Times* science columnist and author Natalie Angier (2007) says, in *The Canon*, that the cell "is surely the greatest invention in the history of life on this planet" (p. 188), an opinion that Mr. Mason can pose to his students in this way:

> *One famous science writer believes that the cell is the greatest invention in the history on earth. Are her lights out upstairs or is she sane? Why?*

The essential idea, of course, is that the endless splitting of cells, as Angier (2007) points out, is how molecular life carries on; it's the very essence of life. This is one reason, at least, why students ought to know how and why cells work. It truly is a big idea but one that leaves room for debate—as well as, one would hope, room for Mr. Mason to cover the material about cell structure and regeneration.

Then there is the problem of the format of the discussion itself, the IRE model of recitation that students instantly recognize as that familiar teacher game called "What's on my mind?" If Mr. Mason were to begin with an essential idea or engaging question, then he might let some silence settle in, or ask for some informal writing on the topic, before inviting student responses. He could ask Category B questions that shape understanding and, when needed, rely on Category A questions to check facts and cover the particulars of the curriculum. This plan would signal to students that this class episode is not a recitation but a genuine discussion, one where the discussants are expected to go further into the topic, using the surface level facts to support their opinions and reflections.

Mr. Mason could use Wait Times 1 and 2 to encourage students to elaborate and refine their thoughts, and he could draw upon his understanding of the dynamics of discussion through the predominance of authentic questions, lots of uptake coupled with levels of evaluation, and challenges geared to his understanding of what are appropriate cognitive challenges for individuals. When students ask good questions, he could use them as points of instruction. "Would everything in the curriculum guide be covered?" one might ask. "Wrong question," I would say, knowing that covering the curriculum by talking at students or holding recitations doesn't ensure any significant amount of genuine learning anyway. But when instruction is based on how minds work and how hearts engage with learning, far more is learned about curriculum and, more important, about the joys of learning.

Supporting Engaged Readers

*C*armen, a sixteen-year-old high school junior, is generally considered a good student; her teachers report that she is "diligent" and "conscientious" in her study skills. But she says that reading in school is hard. It takes her a lot of time, especially when she has to go beyond reading for surface facts or simple plot lines. Higher-level reading challenges her. When she has to read between the lines or apply what she reads to situations outside the text, she struggles. She doesn't know why; she figures that she just wasn't cut out to be a very good reader. Some people just aren't very good readers, and she's one of them, she says. If she didn't have to read for school, she probably wouldn't read at all, except for magazines.

In Carmen's classes, teachers assign reading every day:

- In biology, Mr. G makes her read a section of the chapter for each class; he has the reading schedule all worked out for the semester so she just has to look at that to know what to read each night. He never tells in advance what the reading is going to be about; he just says "Look on the schedule for tonight's reading." He starts off every class with a quiz on the reading, and then he goes over the answers before students start their labs.

- In government, Mrs. B puts the next day's assignment on the chalkboard and students write it down before they leave class. Usually, the reading is part of a chapter, but sometimes she passes out an article to read or something from the Internet. She says things like, "For tomorrow, you'll read *about the executive branch of the federal government. Complete the even questions in the book after you read that section. Full sentences please."*

- *English is much the same. After the class has talked about what's going on in one of the novels, Ms. J tells them to keep going with the reading, up to page such and such by tomorrow. She usually says things like, "Pay close attention to how the author describes the setting in the town," or "Be ready to discuss the imagery."*

In many respects, Carmen is a typical high school student who has typical experiences with reading. She is forming an opinion of herself as a reader based on those experiences, and it is not a positive opinion. She thinks that she is not a good reader, and she avoids reading unless it's forced on her. She knows college reading is going to be even harder, and she's scared that she'll flunk out because she won't be able to do it all, or do it very well. Her teachers assign reading and then check her on it— which *is* their job, she figures—but still, reading never seems to get any easier: in fact, it gets harder when it's on a new subject or something she's never heard of. She wishes she could be back in elementary school because teachers there helped her read; she remembers how they actually taught her how to read different kinds of books, and she believed that she was a pretty good reader then. But in high school, she's learned that it's not the teachers' job to teach students how to read books; their job is to teach their subjects. If you can't read, that's your problem, she heard one say.

In many respects, Carmen's teachers are typical too. They assign reading every day and hold her accountable for completing the assignments— by giving quizzes and tests and by having her write answers to questions. When they have class discussions, many of Carmen's classmates don't understand the reading or give up trying to do it in the first place. (Of course, a fair number of students don't try very hard either.) And so class discussions too often amount to the teachers telling everyone what the reading is about or resorting to calling on the students who get it. Sometimes Carmen and her peers work in groups discussing the reading, and "That's OK," she says, "*if* there's a good reader in the group."

Then there are the quizzes and the unit tests. She tries to understand what she reads but always resorts to simply memorizing what she thinks will be on the quizzes and tests—and then promptly forgets most of it soon after. In English, she has taken to reading what an Internet site says about the story or novel she has been assigned and then restating what she finds out in different words on her papers; she hates having to do that because she knows it's dishonest, but it seems to be the only way to get by. She can't wait for summer because she won't have to read anything at all.

Carmen is one of an increasing number of students who, according to Marge Scherer (2005) editor of the journal *Educational Leadership* "say they don't like to read, read only when they have to, or don't read at all" (p. 7). If Carmen's school day sounds familiar, it should, for it is repeated tens of thousands of times in our schools: Teachers in all subjects approach reading in much the same way. They assign a text (chapter, article, fiction) to be read, they attach accountability to completing the reading (e.g., answering comprehension questions or taking quizzes), and often, they have class "discussions" based on the reading. What they hope will be an engaging discussion inevitably turns out to be a teacher-driven effort to cover the reading and move on.

Yet, 70 percent of the student population struggles with reading (Alliance for Excellent Education, 2004, p. 10). As reported by the Alliance, students struggle, not because they cannot read, but because they cannot understand what they read:

> Most . . . struggling readers can *read* words accurately, but they do not *comprehend* what they read, for a variety of reasons. For some, the problem is that they do not yet read words with enough fluency to facilitate comprehension. Others can read accurately and quickly enough for comprehension to take place, but they lack the strategies to help them comprehend what they read. Such strategies include the ability to grasp the gist of a text, to notice and repair misconceptions, and to change tactics based on the purposes of reading. Other struggling readers may have learned these strategies but have difficulty using them because they have only practiced using them with a limited range of texts and in a limited range of circumstances. Specifically, they may not be able to generalize their strategies to content-area literacy tasks and lack instruction in and knowledge of strategies specific to particular subject areas, such as math, science, and history. (p. 9)

Assigning reading is not the same as helping students read, and expecting them to respond to reading is not the same as helping them to respond. We assign reading, conduct class discussions on the reading, and then assess students' understanding of the reading with the intent of promoting student achievement. It would only make sense, then, to be deliberate in supporting students as readers: By analogy, if science or math teachers expect students to interpret graphs for science or math, they typically help students understand graphs; if they expect students to understand charts in textbooks, they support their efforts there as well. Why shouldn't the same be true of supporting students as readers? Research on reading comprehension clearly shows that student achievement rises when we help students understand the texts we assign (Biancarosa, 2005*, p. 17). If we systematically support students as readers, over time, they learn more. What may take up some time early on is made up for later because less time has to be spent on reteaching and reviewing the material. Teaching reading across the curriculum, in the ways outlined below, helps students read better and raises their achievement (Benjamin, 2007*)—and we don't need to become reading specialists to support their reading.

ENGAGED READING

By *reading*, I mean understanding texts. I do not mean print awareness, letter-sound correspondence, word recognition, or fluency, though these other aspects of reading may very well challenge some students and certainly do impact comprehension, even among skilled readers who read challenging texts. But when skilled readers encounter a difficult text, they read with a purpose, they read on and below the surface, and they read strategically. Most important, they read for understanding.

Reading for genuine understanding goes beyond merely answering questions, as we saw in the vignette on Carmen's experiences with school reading at the start of this chapter. If we are going to support readers in our classes, we need to know just what we mean by *engaged reading*—so that we can easily and convincingly explain to our students why and how particular reading strategies will help them become better readers. Recall that one of the conditions of flow experiences is that people have a clear goal. Thus, if we can clarify the goal of a reading strategy, if we can say just how it improves comprehension such that students understand why they are learning the strategy, then we are more likely to make the reading experience engaging.

So then, what *is* engaged reading? Simply put, it is reading for genuine understanding. But we have to deconstruct *genuine understanding* in order to get to a workable definition that makes sense to developing readers, and for that, I find the work of two teachers and reading researchers invaluable. Ellin Keene (2008) shows us what happens in the minds of readers and in their lives when they read to understand; Sheridan Blau (2003) illuminates for us the intellectual and emotional dispositions readers experience when they become engaged readers. Combined, Keene's and Blau's work provides us with a rich and comprehensive understanding of engaged reading. (I encourage you to read their wonderful books yourself, for I surely do not do them justice in the abbreviated accounts below.)

Reading for genuine understanding, as Keene (2008) writes, involves a rich variety of *intellectual outcomes.* In reading fiction, readers may develop character or author empathy, predict events in the chronology, appreciate textual aesthetics, recognize themes and symbols, and revise understanding while reading. In reading nonfiction, readers may appropriate writers' techniques for their own writing, apply learning in new contexts, connect new knowledge with existing knowledge, compare and contrast concepts as well as see causal relationships among events, and revise understandings as new information presents itself. Additionally, Keene describes understanding in terms of what *happens in readers' lives* when they read fiction and expository texts. For example, they fervently lose themselves in the world of the text, they reflect on ideas and talk them over with others, they extend their reading interests to new texts and genres, they savor the emotional experiences of reading, and they remember well what they have read (pp. 24–27). Keene's model illuminates what happens in students' minds and in their lives when they become engaged readers.

Engaged reading also includes the intellectual and emotional dispositions—or traits—that competent readers (of all ages) experience when they read for understanding. Blau (2003) calls these traits *dimensions of performative literacy*, and they complement Keene's model of comprehension by underscoring the habits of mind needed for deeply engaged reading:

- A capacity for sustained, focused attention, whereby readers invest the time and attention necessary to understanding a text
- Willingness to suspend closure, in which readers expect temporary confusion as they read, leaving themselves open for eventual clarity
- Willingness to take risks—for example, to offer an alternative reading or an unorthodox interpretation of a text
- Tolerance for failure, by which readers persevere in reading and rereading, knowing that reading a difficult text is, well, difficult, and may well result in bewilderment after all
- Tolerance for ambiguity, paradox, and uncertainty during reading, coupled with the capacity to try to resolve mysterious issues
- An intellectual generosity that allows readers to suspend disbelief in alternative perspectives while also entertaining the possibility that they may learn something valuable by being open-minded as they read
- Metacognitive awareness, whereby readers reflect on their understanding of a text as they read, reread when necessary, and rely on self-correction when they encounter comprehension challenges (pp. 211–214)

When combined, Keene's and Blau's views of reading provide us with a rich definition of engaged reading that can guide the support we give to students throughout the reading process. I've found that having a comprehensive and dynamic definition of reading like this helps me to explain to students why various reading strategies will help them become stronger readers of a variety of texts. I am making a distinction here between *teaching strategies* (what teachers do to support readers) and *reading strategies* (what readers do to understand texts) so that, as a *teaching strategy*, we explain why and how particular *reading strategies* help students become better readers. As you will see below, for example, it is one thing to ask students to complete anticipation guides without showing them how doing so will help them read better—and quite another to show students how doing anticipation guides will help them become more imaginative readers of fiction or more logical readers of expository texts.

TRINAL (THREE-PART) APPROACHES TO READING

There are three phases of reading texts that commonly appear in classrooms across the curriculum:

- Before reading
- During reading
- After reading

The Commission on Reading of the National Council of Teachers of English (2004*) writes that teachers provide effective reading instruction when they "teach before-, during-, and after-reading strategies for constructing meaning of written language, including demonstrations and think alouds." Trinal approaches are also recommended by the National Reading Panel (2000*) as having significant effects on reading achievement (pp. 4–162).

Reading instruction includes both reading strategies and teaching strategies, as explained in the previous section. According to the research (Egan, 1997*; Garner, 2008*; Olson & Land, 2007*), we get the best results with reading instruction when we teach *cognitive reading strategies* through teaching strategies that include *scaffolding* and *modeling*. *Cognitive strategies instruction* (e.g., anticipation guides and graphic organizers) consistently produce the most success, as noted, for example, by the National Reading Panel Report: "When readers are given cognitive strategies instruction, they make significant gains on measures of reading comprehension" (International Reading Association, 2002,* p. 13). Always explaining to students why particular reading strategies will help them, we *scaffold* cognitive strategies instruction by helping students practice reading strategies

with support that is gradually withdrawn as students become more independent. We might, for example, explain why good readers separate facts
from inferences when reading and then demonstrate how to separate facts
from inferences; as students become more self-sufficient, we take a back
seat in the process and gradually shift responsibility to students as they
become more skilled at separating facts from inferences (Olson & Land,
2007*). *Modeling our own reading processes* for students makes visible otherwise private aspects of comprehension by talking aloud as we read; we
show how we overcome reading challenges, such as what to do when
we encounter unknown words or when we lose track of meaning, and we
demystify (and democratize) the whole business of reading difficult texts
(Schoenbach et al., 1999*).

When we promote reading through trinal approaches, we support
less-skilled readers by presenting, modeling, and integrating the reading
habits of skilled readers, as researchers Michael Pressley and Karen R.
Harris (2001) point out:

> Skilled readers are more active than unskilled readers. . . . Before
> reading, they are likely to preview a text, sizing up what's in it and
> making decisions about how they are going to read it (e.g., decid-
> ing which sections are most relevant to their purposes and opting
> to read those more carefully). During reading, they adjust reading
> speed depending on a number of factors, including text relevance,
> density, and level of interest. Good readers sometimes choose to
> reread especially difficult or relevant sections of a text. After read-
> ing, good readers may reflect on the reading, deciding which parts
> of text are worth remembering and thinking about how they
> might use ideas from this text in the future. (p. 466)

In the following sections, I discuss representative strategies for supporting readers across the curriculum before, during, and after reading.
There are scores of comprehension strategies we could choose from (see,
for example, The Literacy Web, 2008); I shall select but a few. While many
excellent approaches have proved effective in schools, the authors of
Reading Next remind us that "no one approach is necessarily better than
another; the ideal intervention will tap more than one comprehension
instructional approach" (Alliance for Excellent Education, 2004*, p. 13).

Before-Reading Comprehension Strategies

Since learners' brains need to make connections between new and existing information in order for the new information to make sense, students

need help *activating prior knowledge*. The more they know what they know before reading, the more they comprehend. Many students don't realize that, however. *Anticipation guides* can help make connections—once students understand why anticipation guides help them read better, they respond to statements that anticipate the reading in some way and through that process make connections between what they already know about a topic and what the guide suggests may be in the reading. There are many types of anticipation guides, and here is one that might be used with Martin Luther King's "Letter From a Birmingham Jail" in a humanities or history class.

CHECK YOUR RATING FOR EACH STATEMENT:

AGREE	DISAGREE	CAN'T DECIDE	
_____	_____	_____	People have the right to disobey some laws.
AGREE	DISAGREE	CAN'T DECIDE	
_____	_____	_____	It's OK to act publicly against a rule that you think is wrong.
AGREE	DISAGREE	CAN'T DECIDE	
_____	_____	_____	It's better to go to jail than to ignore your conscience.
AGREE	DISAGREE	CAN'T DECIDE	
_____	_____	_____	I would feel OK about taking part in a sit-down protest at school.
AGREE	DISAGREE	CAN'T DECIDE	
_____	_____	_____	Injustice anywhere is a threat to justice everywhere.
AGREE	DISAGREE	CAN'T DECIDE	
_____	_____	_____	If someone hits me, I should hit them back.

This anticipation guide invites students to think about some of the issues raised in King's letter—blind obedience to unjust laws, nonviolent protest, following one's conscience, and social justice. After making their choices, students discuss why they marked as they did, and we use their value judgments as a way of introducing the reading. It's important to approach the students' values as unresolved tensions: Under what circumstances *would* it be OK to break the law? What issues *would* compel you to spend time in jail? What public acts *might* be OK to take part in if you needed to protest something?

Other anticipation guides might ask students to decide if statements are true or false, or if they can be answered yes/no, +/−, and so on. The value of these guides lies in the expectation that once having made their decisions, students can defend and elaborate upon their decisions. Consequently, the discussion that follows the exercise is what matters most in preparing them for the reading.

Sentence starters invite students to follow a line of thinking that anticipates the substance or themes of the reading. Once again, we need to clarify for students why sentence starters can support them as readers and then demonstrate how to work with the starters so they can write them on their own. Here, for example, is a set of sentence starters that might be used with middle school math students preparing to read about predicting from patterns:

- When I hear the word *pattern*, I think about . . .
- An example of a pattern that I know about is . . .
- If something *breaks a pattern*, that means it . . .

Another type of before-reading sentence starter accesses students' prior knowledge about the specific content of the reading, as in the following example from a high school chemistry reading on gases, liquids, and solids in the context of global warming:

- Gasses, liquids, and solids differ in that . . .
- When I hear the phrase *polar melting*, I think about . . .
- If someone were to tell me that glacial melting is more serious than polar melting, I would say that's because . . .
- When ice melts, it . . .

Other sentence starters may be used more generally to activate prior knowledge or to assist with setting reading goals, as Olson and Land (2007*) suggest.

Tapping prior knowledge:

- I already know that . . .
- This reminds me of . . .
- This relates to . . .

Planning and goal setting:

- My purpose is . . .
- My top priority is . . .
- To accomplish my goal, I plan to . . .

Visual tools are especially helpful for organizing thinking before reading, such as the way comparison and contrast tools separate ideas into categories. As a teaching strategy for working with visual tools, we explain to students how the tools support their reading, use the tool with a real text, and then support students as they work with tools on their own (or collaboratively). In the following example from high school American history, students preparing to read about the Civil War were asked to write, in Venn diagram fashion, what they thought the differences were between the North and the South as well as what they had in common.

North	Both	South

Many visual-tool books are available to support students' reading (e.g., Burke, 2002; Drapeau, 2008; Hyerle, 2008). Burke's (2002) "decision tree," for example, was helpful to an American government class about to read an article on the death penalty (this is a variation on Burke's model):

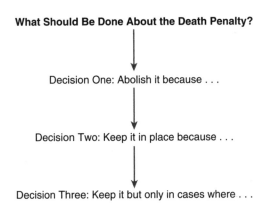

What Should Be Done About the Death Penalty?

Decision One: Abolish it because . . .

Decision Two: Keep it in place because . . .

Decision Three: Keep it but only in cases where . . .

During-Reading Comprehension Strategies

During-reading comprehension strategies help readers keep track of information during the reading process. As *metacognitive* activities, they help readers monitor their understanding while comprehension builds. Too often, challenged readers never stop to ask if they are actually getting it; instead, they just plunge ahead until they reach that inevitable point of saying, "I have no idea what this is all about!"

The *KWL strategy* (i.e., What do I *know?* What do I *want* to know? What did I *learn?*) actually begins as a prereading *anticipation* guide activity that students continue to rely on during reading. It is usually used to prepare for reading informational texts because the focus is on what is to be learned. It generally looks like this:

What I Know	What I Want to Know	What I Learned

If the KWL were to be used by a student reading King's "Letter From a Birmingham Jail," it might be tweaked for students to record their learning *while* they read:

What I Know	What I Want to Know	What I Learned
Dr. King was a hero.	What did he do in Birmingham?	Dr. King went there to help out. He was
He did what he believed.	Why was he in jail?	put in jail because he broke the law but he felt he had to
Birmingham is in the South somewhere.	What is a sit in?	because he thought the law was unjust.
Sometimes you have to stand up for what you believe in.	Why didn't the police help the blacks more?	The police were just part of the problem and didn't help the blacks.
	Why is this a famous letter?	I still don't know why it's famous or what
It's wrong to break the law.	What was the president doing about the civil rights?	the president was doing. I still don't think I could go to jail
I would not want to go to jail for anything.		for anything but I understand why Dr. King did.

During-reading *sentence starters* help readers track and record what they are learning while reading, and they can help monitor cognitive understanding as it develops. Here are some examples used by Olson and Land (2007*) in their research.

Asking questions:

- I wonder why . . .
- What if . . .
- How come . . .

Predicting:

- I'll bet that . . .
- I think . . .
- If ____, then _____

Visualizing:

- I can picture . . .
- In my mind I see . . .
- If this were a movie . . .

Making connections:

- This reminds me of . . .
- I experienced this once when . . .
- I can relate to this because . . .

Forming interpretations:

- What this means to me is . . .
- I think this represents . . .
- The idea I'm getting is . . .

Monitoring:

- I got lost here because . . .
- I need to reread the part where . . .
- I know I'm on the right track because . . .

Clarifying:

- To understand better, I need to know more about . . .
- Something that is still not clear is . . .
- I'm guessing what this means, but I need to . . .

Students can use many visual tools during reading. Venn diagrams, as previously discussed, can be filled in *while* reading as a way of recording information while it's fresh, and decision trees can be elaborated upon as students learn more while reading. *Timelines* help students keep track of the sequence of events, as in this case where a student used a timeline to record the melting of a glacier.

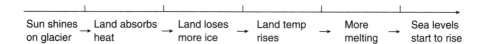

Sun shines on glacier → Land absorbs heat → Land loses more ice → Land temp rises → More melting → Sea levels start to rise

Visual ways to *graph arguments* can support students trying to follow the logical connections in written arguments. Here is a visual tool that can be used to record the support for two sides of an argument.

Claim A:

   Support #1 for Claim A:

      Most important details about Claim A:

   Support #2 for Claim A:

      Most important details about Claim A:

   Support #3 for Claim A:

      Most important details about Claim A:

Claim B:

   Support #1 for Claim B:

      Most important details about Claim B:

   Support #2 for Claim B:

      Most important details about Claim B:

   Support #3 for Claim B:

      Most important details about Claim B:

After-Reading Comprehension Strategies

After-reading strategies help readers look back and reflect on the content of what they've read. If readers don't "do something with" (Hashimoto, 1991, p. 23) what they've learned from a text, then it's pretty certain that it won't be remembered. Many teachers give quizzes to find out whether or not the students actually did the reading and also to learn what students understand or don't understand. Although quizzes can be used to guide us in reteaching concepts or in differentiating instruction for those who need it, too often the quiz scores are merely recorded and then configured into student grades rather than used systematically to guide further instruction. For after-reading comprehension checks, however, alternatives to quizzes are plentiful, and they can more readily be used to guide instruction because they provide more useful information than quizzes. Used instructionally, after-reading strategies help readers synthesize information, make more connections between what they've read and what the reading makes them think about, clarify their understandings, and elaborate on what they've learned.

Teachers often have students go back to their before-reading *anticipation guides* to reconsider their responses in light of new insights. For example, one student studying King's "Letter From a Birmingham Jail" commented from the anticipation guide (see p. 94) that if someone hits him, he should hit them back because that is what the Bible said to do. After reading the letter, however, he wrote that there "might be times when not hitting back would be wiser," though he would "still have some problems with that tactic." When students return to the anticipation guides to revisit their original opinions, they integrate the ideas of the reading into their own thinking about, or rethinking of, the issues.

Sentence starters can likewise be revisited to see if students want to change their responses in light of what they've read. For example, the student who originally wrote "When I hear the phrase 'polar melting,' I think about what's going to happen to all the polar bears who'll die," then wrote, ". . . but now I mostly think about how much worse things are going to be because the glaciers are melting at a faster rate and that's the bigger threat from global warming."

Sentence starters written during reading can be looked at again for what the reader *now* knows about the content after reading, as in the case of one student who first wrote, "If this was a movie, it would be a disaster film about rising sea levels in California" and then revised it to read, "If this was a movie, it would last a really long time because of how slow the sea rises in global warming, no one notices it until it's too late. The movie would have to compress time a lot to get the plot moving along." Returning to anticipation guides and to sentence starters takes no extra teacher preparation; the students themselves do all the thinking work on their original guides. The real payoff lies in the ways students are supported in extending, revising, and elaborating their thinking in light of what they have learned.

Other sentence starters that are particularly aimed at after-reading help students with a number of cognitive tasks, as noted by Olson and Land (2007*).

Summarizing:

- The basic gist is . . .
- The key information is . . .
- In a nutshell, this says that . . .

Adopting an alignment:

- The character I most identify with is . . .
- I really got into this story when . . .
- I can relate to this author because . . .

Revising meaning:

- At first I thought _____, but now I . . .
- My latest thought about this is . . .
- I'm getting a different picture here because . . .

Analyzing the author's craft:

- A golden line for me is . . .
- This word/phrase stands out for me because . . .
- I like how the author uses _____ to show . . .

Reflecting and relating:

- So, the big idea is . . .
- A conclusion I'm drawing is . . .
- This is relevant to my life because . . .

Evaluating:

- I like/don't like _____ because . . .
- This could be more effective if . . .
- The most important message is . . . (p. 281)

Visual tools such as those presented previously can also be reused. The KWL strategy, for instance, can be extended by adding a fourth column titled WHAT I NOW THINK ABOUT _____, where students write in their reflections, on, say, civil disobedience, patterns in math, or global warming.

What I Know	What I Want to Know	What I Learned	What I Now Think About

One of the most powerful cognitive strategies to recommend is the *summary,* for writing a summary forces readers to put into their own words a synthesis of what they understand, and it forces them to return to the reading to check details. Most important, summarizing enhances achievement (Marzano, Pickering, & Pollock, 2001*). In the KWL visual tool, a section can be added where students write summaries of what they read.

What I Know	What I Want to Know	What I Learned
Dr. King was a hero.	What did he do in Birmingham?	Dr. King went there to help out. He was
He did what he believed.	Why was he in jail?	put in jail because he broke the law but he felt he had to
Birmingham is in the South somewhere.	What is a sit in?	because he thought the law was unjust.
Sometimes you have to stand up for what you believe in.	Why didn't the police help the blacks more?	The police were just part of the problem and didn't help the blacks.
It's wrong to break the law.	Why is this a famous letter? What was the president doing about the civil rights?	I still don't know why it's famous or what the president was doing. I still don't
I would not want to go to jail for anything.		think I could go to jail for anything but I understand why Dr. King did.

Summary:

Likewise, a *summary block* as well as an *allegiance block* can easily be added to the argument graph.

Claim A:

Support #1 for Claim A:

Most important details about Claim A:

Support #2 for Claim A:

Most important details about Claim A:

Support #3 for Claim A:

Most important details about Claim A:

Claim B:

Support #1 for Claim B:

Most important details about Claim B:

Support #2 for Claim B:

Most important details about Claim B:

Support #3 for Claim B:

Most important details about Claim B:

Summary of Claim A:

Summary of Claim B:

The claim I support and why:

Simply assigning summaries doesn't mean students will know how to write them, of course. They need direct instruction (e.g., modeling, scaffolding practice). *Summary frames* (Hill & Flynn, 2006; Marzano et al., 2001), for instance, give students structures for writing summaries specifically geared for discrete genres like arguments and narratives. Here are frame questions for an argument summary.

- What information does the author present that leads her to make a claim?
- What claim does the author make about a problem or situation? What does she assert about it?
- What examples or explanations does the author present to support her claim?
- Does the author present a restriction on the claim? (Hill & Flynn, 2006, p. 125)

One final visual tool—*color coding*—has strong support in the research because it helps the brain to identify categories of information in a text. Olson and Land (2007*) recommend color coding argumentative essays in order to make visible different types of statements in an analytical essay:

Teachers designated colors for three types of assertions that make up an analytical essay. For example, they might say, "Plot summary reiterates what is obvious and known in a text. It is *yellow* because it's kind of superficial and lightweight. We sometimes want some plot summary to orient our reader to the facts, but we want to keep plot summary to a minimum. Commentary is *blue* because it goes beneath the surface of things to look at the deeper meaning. Commentary occurs when we move from what the text says to what it means. It's your opinion, interpretations, insights, and 'Ahas.' Commentary goes beyond summary to interpret the significance of something. Supporting detail is *green* because it's what glues together plot summary and commentary. It's your evidence to support your claims. In writing a successful essay, it is especially important to quote from the text to provide evidence for your ideas." (p. 284)

I recommend color coding as an after-reading strategy rather than a during-reading strategy because it is hard for most readers to identify the structural elements of discourse while grappling with the ideas. Going back over the text after reading to color code allows the mind to work on one plane—at the level of statement types—separate from working at the plane of idea comprehension. Some teachers use color coding to help students identify facts and inferences, showing and telling statements, and certain grammatical structures such as passive and active voice and other stylistic variations.

CARMEN AND SCHOOL READING

Predictability considerations about engaged reading would include the following:

- *Mind:* The trinal approach fosters connections with prior knowledge that students make themselves; students actively construct meaning, often in social ways, and often finding pleasure in reading that has been made more accessible.
- *Heart:* Reading comprehension strategies (e.g., anticipation guides) often ask students to examine their own values and become attuned to others' values; they encourage students to see how the little stories of their own lives relate to the big stories of history, literature, philosophy, and so on; and because they force students to pay greater attention while reading, they promote mindful reading.

- *Flow:* Reading goals become clearer because reading becomes more purposeful; during-reading comprehension strategies provide immediate feedback relevant to performance; and, hopefully, reading becomes more pleasurable.

Using the engaged reading perspective developed in this chapter, let's look at what Carmen's experiences with reading in her high school classes might have been.

Carmen's biology teacher assigns reading every day. Mr. G often poses ethical dilemmas that get Carmen thinking about some aspect of science that she's going to read about. Yesterday, in fact, Mr. G had students write a sentence starter that began, "I think the most important part of the human body is . . . because . . ." before they were to read the chapter on cell life, where the claim is made that the cell is the most important element of the human body because it reproduces itself. Carmen then reads that chapter to confirm or disconfirm her hypothesis that DNA is the most important part. She comes to school the next day still convinced that it is DNA in spite of what the book said. She even gets into a heated discussion with Mr. G over that, and he plays devil's advocate all along. She likes that part of the class; she feels engaged.

Then, before he assigns the next night's reading (an article from the Internet that examines synthetic cell production from three perspectives—a scientist, a clergyman, and a legislator), he poses yet another sentence starter that gets her thinking about the ethics of synthetic cell production. This time, however, she is also asked to write up a "Think in Threes" visual tool (Burke, 2002, p. 102) that compares the three views. Again, she reads with a purpose, and again, she returns to school the next day ready to examine the ethical issue from multiple perspectives. Because she thinks about the controversies before she reads, and because she fills in the visual tool while she reads, Carmen is able to write in her biology notebook a full-page response to the sentence starter, "Before I read the article about synthetic cell production, I thought . . . but now I think . . ."

It should come as no surprise, then, to learn that, over time, Carmen's achievement in biology improves. She now finds that she understands biology better—and she remembers more. She plans to read a book Mr. G. recommended to her called The Lives of a Cell, *(Thomas, 1978) during the summer vacation.*

Supporting
Engaged Writers

Courtney, a second-year student in my Introduction to Poetry and Drama class at the university, entered the course skeptical about poetry. In an interview about her previous experiences with poetry, she told me that she thought most poetry was hard to read, that she struggled to "figure it out," and that writing papers about poetry was never easy or enjoyable. She said that she had to write about poetry in high school, and she did, but it was always in essays where "you'd latch onto some single main point, like the death theme in a poem, and then go on to give three reasons why that was important and on and on," she said. She didn't like to write about poetry, she said, because she didn't understand it very well and because what she wrote always seemed so stilted and formal. She signed up for my course because, as an English major, she felt she had to give poetry one more shot because she might have to teach it herself one day when she became a teacher. She made me wonder, was Courtney's problem actually *reading* poetry, or was it the way she had to write about it in school? I find that it's often hard to separate reading problems from writing problems— what appears to be a writing problem often results from reading problems. With Courtney, it was hard to separate the two, but when I asked her to talk more about the kind of writing she did in school before college, it soon became apparent that the problem had to do with writing.

She said that, in middle and high school, 95 percent of her writing was the thesis-driven essay, in all subjects except science where there were lab reports. Research papers, Courtney said, *were just five-paragraph essays expanded into a few more pages, and all you have to do is prove your point with facts and quotes, make sure your grammar is good, and use the right bibliography style, MLA.*

A lot of the time, teachers made us outline before we wrote, so we could get our ideas clear and organized. Sometimes I had good ideas on a topic but they wouldn't fit into the outline so I just left them out. Sometimes I didn't have like just one point to prove but just some questions about a topic, like when I wrote about torture laws and I actually ended up wondering if some torture might be necessary sometimes, but I had to keep writing that all torture is wrong, no shades of gray in essayville. I tried to avoid saying something that didn't fit with the thesis; I didn't want to get marked down for going off topic or for getting sidetracked or whatever. Some college teachers are like that too, but not all, thank god.

A prospective teacher herself, Courtney said that she realizes that high school teachers are under great pressure for students to do well on mandated proficiency tests and so the thesis-driven essay is the main kind of writing done in school. I said that I thought this kind of writing is important in some school tasks, such as essay exams, and she agreed, but she felt strongly that it did not allow her freedom to express her ideas or experiment with ideas in her writing. She complained, too, about the use of scoring rubrics in high school:

We had writing rubrics for everything we wrote for our classes and they were all about the same—content, organization, style, grammar, basically—so you know how it's going to be graded. That's OK, I suppose—better than teachers who grade stuff and you never know why it's a C or a B or whatever. But the rubrics seemed more important that our writing or our ideas. Teachers would say things like "Wow, Courtney, you have some great thoughts here on blah blah blah, but sorry, your thesis isn't clear and your grammar sucks: C." I had friends who were afraid to write anything if they didn't have a rubric 'cause they were worried about doing something wrong right from the start. Personally, I hate rubrics.

I was not surprised at what Courtney told me about her experiences with writing because I had heard many similar sentiments from other students. For many, "school writing" was little more than formulaic essays that we all know too well and that are the mainstay of proficiency tests. The formulaic essay, in fact, has become the unfortunate standard for good writing beginning in middle schools and extending to higher education. In most schools, "good writing" is a *noun phrase* because it is seen as a product, with definable and quantifiable characteristics that easily lend themselves to scoring rubrics. If asked what good writing is, students, many teachers, and administrators respond in the ways Courtney did—one main point stated in the first paragraph, X number of supporting details, X number of paragraphs, no digressions, X number of references, outlines where, as Courtney put it, "if you have an A, you gotta have a B." "Good writing" proves a point with good evidence, is clear and correct, and for many, is also impersonal (students are still advised to never use "I" or contractions in academic writing, regardless of audience and purpose).

I must agree that this *is* good writing—in certain academic and nonacademic contexts and for certain purposes and audiences. It's hard to be successful anywhere if you can't state one point clearly and then explain why that point is true or persuade someone to believe it. I'm proud that I've taught many writers to write well this way without using formulas. But I am saddened that it has become virtually the *only* honored form of writing that so many young people practice, for it does not easily lend itself to *engaged writing.* Engaged writing takes as its syntax a *verb phrase*—engaged *writing*—rather than a noun phrase. Engaged writing is something writers *do*; it's not a product they end up with.

ENGAGED WRITING

Engaged writing challenges the dominant writing paradigm in schools because instead of using writing to *prove learning,* writers write to discover and revise learning. Essentially, writing *is* learning. Writing used for learning, writing done to explore ideas and push the frontiers of understanding is not considered "school writing" in Courtney's mind or in the minds of her peers. Yet, as the research by Sommers and Saltz (2004*) makes clear, the product view of writing does not prepare students well for the paradigm shift they must undergo when colleges and universities expect writing for higher-order purposes. This research shows that when university students write, they are expected to exercise various modes of authentic thinking, called "experiments," where they "question, evaluate, and interpret ideas they are trying to comprehend for the first time" (p. 128). Students who engage in such writing describe the experience as something approximating flow, which brings with it an astonishing sense of satisfaction and achievement, a

> pride of accomplishment . . . the joy of holding in their hands the
> physical representation of the thinking that they have learned

something in-depth. . . . "You get this high, seeing that you have actually produced something, something that you actually care about . . . your writing is improving, and your thinking is improving, and you can see it, and hold it in your hands." (p. 129)

Engaging writing, like engaging reading, takes writers to places they don't anticipate, it surprises them with what it reveals to them, it explores learning and nurtures curiosity, and it dialogues with ideas and feelings in ways that resemble good conversation with friends, mentors, and people we trust. As an example, here is a student teacher writing in his learning journal about his experiences in his assigned school. Note how his writing articulates a compelling clash of personal values as he probes below the surface of his daily experiences and professional beliefs.

September 27: The more I see of teachers in this school, the more I hear them speak, the more I see them in action, my radical viewpoint of education is further reinforced. The more I sit in the classroom and watch children, the more I teach in a classroom with someone else's structure, the more I learn of just what happens in the school, my radical viewpoint of education is further reinforced. My classes at _____ reinforce my views; the more I see of student teachers who are taking the same classes as I am, and who become typical teachers once they get into their schools in the morning, the more reinforcement I receive. (Nystrand & Weiderspiel, 1977, p. 114).

Engaged writers wrestle with ideas *while they write.* In the next example, a high school science student writes in his "Neuron Notes" about his understanding of osmosis. Notice his tentative voice, his doubts, and his authentic spirit of curiosity.

Osmosis is to do with water and cells. Osmosis is the absorbing of water by cells, or pass through. I don't know what it does exactly once it's inside. Osmosis is not the only way, but the one that is used the most is diffusion. I would like to know where they got a name like osmosis for it? Osmosis is different than any other form, but still gets the job done. When it occurs, water actually passes through a membrane so as to equalize the amount on both sides of the cell or whatever kind of membrane it is. (Tierney, 2002, pp. 15–16)

Engaging writing carries with it the same habits of mind and heart exemplified by engaging reading (see Chapter 8):

- A capacity for sustained, focused attention, whereby readers invest the time and attention necessary to understanding a text
- Willingness to suspend closure on ideas, in which writers who encounter confusion as they write see it as a natural part of composing
- Willingness to take risks—for example, risks in thinking alternatively (intellectual risks) as well as risks in expressing themselves (stylistic risks)
- Tolerance for failure, by which writers persevere in the act of writing, while knowing that all writing is drafting and subject to further drafting and that, at some point, the draft may just have to be abandoned. They do not, as one student put it, "have their guts tied up in it."
- Tolerance for discovered ambiguity, paradox, and uncertainty while writing, along with the desire to write one's way through problematic or puzzling issues
- An intellectual generosity that allows writers to try on alternative perspectives for what they might learn about their own perspectives
- Metacognitive awareness, whereby writers reflect on their writing as they write, rewrite when necessary, try alternative strategies (e.g., nonlinear ways of outlining [Burke, 2002; Murray, 2002] or freewriting [Elbow, 1981])

With these habits of mind and heart entrenched in their ways of approaching writing tasks, writers come to relish the new understandings that writing may bring about, although they may not always enjoy the hard work that writing entails. In the pages that follow, I examine engaged writing in some detail, focusing on those elements that highlight how school writing can be more engaging.

PURPOSES FOR WRITING

Engaged writers write for real purposes. I don't mean the artificially imposed purposes we see on standardized proficiency tests, such as the writing task included in the assessment for the 2008 *Nation's Report Card:*

Imagine that the article shown below appeared in your local newspaper. Read the article carefully, then write a letter to your principal arguing for or against the proposition that classes at your school should begin and end much later in the day. Be sure to give detailed reasons to support your argument and make it convincing. (National Assessment of Educational Progress, 2008)

Engaged writers explore a *genuine need*—for instance, to understand, put forth, defend, discover, work through, or create something. Below, for example, are some writers writing for such genuine purposes. The first person writes the story of his experiment to discover if a twenty-dollar bill, "placed in the right hand at the right moment, makes things happen":

> I've always wanted to test myself, to establish the weight and worth of a twenty in the world. So last month I took two grand in twenties, rolled them up, and left for New York. I was going to spend three days greasing palms from gate to gate and see what it got me. (Chiarella, 2004, p. 412)

Second, a music student writes to articulate her definition of music:

> The other day in music class, we were asked to write down our definition of what music was. I took a sort of phenomenological viewpoint, and wrote that music depends as much on the listener as the sound which is being created; if the listener hears a certain combination of sounds as music, then it's music. . . . As someone else mentioned in class, music is the "barometer" of our feelings, thoughts, ideals and dreams, perhaps one of the greatest expressions of our higher selves. I think that will be my definition of music, at least for the time being; that which evokes a response from, corresponds to, or is an expression of our "higher selves." (Ambrose, 1987, p. 263)

As a final example, here is teacher Sarah Rider (2005) writing to understand how to work with a white separatist student in her college composition course:

> How could I give William's work the attention it deserved when the thought of his point of view made me feel angry, sick, and sad? How does an instructor, whose work is supposed to be about promoting critical thinking and equal access, resist the temptation to silence a student because she finds his view repugnant?

In authentic writing, it's not hard to find a genuine purpose—if writers have opportunities to explore their beliefs, curiosities, hypotheses, intellectual complexities, emotional conundrums, ethical dilemmas, and textual understandings. To be sure, I do not exclude the more traditional purposes and forms for writing here, such as writing to persuade (e.g., in essays) or writing to inform (e.g., in research papers), for they too can become venues for genuine exploration, as I hope to show below.

When writers grapple with subject matter, such as texts or other forms of data in science and math, the main purpose, as Hashimoto (1991) says, is "to do something with" (p. 23) what has been read or observed, not merely to regurgitate it: "[Students] are often just reporting what they have found instead of trying to say something about what they have found" (p. 167). For example, a good case has been made for summarizing (Marzano et al., 2001; Wormeli, 2004) because summarizing demands that writers do something with information.

AUDIENCES FOR WRITING

For most school writing, teachers take on the familiar role of evaluator, and in that role, they are responsible for both reading and grading a student's writing. Courtney, like most students, played safe with her writing, seldom daring to violate the norms of the rubrics because she knew she would be graded down. In schools where all writing "counts" and where "writing" is defined not as writing-to-learn but as writing-to-prove-learning, teachers become evaluator audiences by default—and students, accordingly, write safely for them, by taking few chances with ideas, style, or structure.

Engaging writing demands an audience that appreciates the tug and pull of ideas as ideas are forming and one that understands that genuine learning is not a tidy and predictable linear process but rather a recursive and messy meaning-construction process. Teachers who regularly do their own writing-to-learn know firsthand that they must be able to express themselves without fear of punishment in the form of grades (one good reason why the brain would downshift). Martin, D'Arcy, Newton, and Parker (1976), in their research on writing and learning, remind us that we must

> make a conscious effort to provide our pupils with an audience which enables them to write what they really think without being constantly criticized about it; for a reader in other words who will pay real regard to the way it looks through their eyes. We believe it is just as important for the teacher to provide this kind of sympathetic audience in subjects such as history, geography, and science as it is in the more traditionally "personal" subjects such as English and religious education. (p. 81)

FORMS OF ENGAGED WRITING

In a sense, this is a misleading heading because any form of writing can become engaging. That is, engaged writing is not about what it looks like on paper or on a screen but rather what a writer does while writing or why a writer decides to write something in the first place rather than talk about it or represent it in some other medium (e.g., drawing). Accordingly, writing a business letter could become exploratory in the drafting stages, as could an e-mail message. Just as conversation with a trusted friend or teacher seems a more likely form of talk to explore ideas in preparation for giving a formal speech, so too can writing in an idea journal lead to more mainstream school genres like the essay and the research paper. But to say that form doesn't matter would be misleading because, by their very characteristics, some forms invite the thinking and stylistic riskiness we associate with writing to learn.

Take the academic essay, but not the one that Courtney describes. Take, instead, the personal essay, the kind you might find in the annual *Best American Essays* or *Best American Magazine Writing* collections. Here, writers instantiate the original French meaning of *essay,* which in its verb form meant *to try* or *to attempt:* They attempt to work out ideas in extended prose that captures their minds at work. In that sense, an essay may be considered an attempt to work out an idea or set of ideas, as did the Renaissance writer Michel de Montaigne, in his *Essais,* in which he expressed his thoughts and speculations on such topics as "Of the Art of Conferring" and "Of Coaching." The line between the personal essay, with its prominent authorial voice and its penchant for self-referential stances, and what some would consider the standard academic essay is thin. For those of us who actually read academic essays, we often find writers who do, in fact, use "I" and other forms of self-recognition; who do, in fact, write about doubts and uncertainties; and who do, often, express the "main point" as complex and multifaceted. It is the ability to write such essays that separates them from less-skilled writers who often struggle to explain just one thing well, as is true for many of our students.

My point is not that we should bar students from writing the personal academic essay because they are developmentally unable to do so; my point is that we should not make the academic essay a dry and regimented form of writing that is antithetical to engaged writing. We should, instead, encourage the intellectual exploration and stylistic and structural innovations that engage students as writers. We should promote the writing of *hybrid essays*—the kind that look like traditional essays but that attempt to wrangle with and articulate newly learned or emergent ideas. Why pretend that all ideas have one main point and three to five supporting ideas? What does that teach people about critical thinking? What are we touting as "good thinking" when we imply that all writing ends up with narrowly defining "main points," little in the way of complexity, and virtually no room for doubt or speculation?

To clarify: Thesis-support essays or essays that put forth one thesis or argumentative premise are important, indeed, essential writing products in schools. But so too are exploratory essays and learning journals that allow writers to examine other, more open-ended, difficult issues and questions, the kind that call for multiple perspectives on a topic or that invite writers to consider alternatives without being forced to promote only one. Here are some invitations to exploratory writing from a literature class:

- How is Prufrock like someone you know, possibly you yourself?
- If you were a character in *The Great Gatsby*, would you have admired Gatsby—or not? Why?
- In the story, "A Jury of Her Peers," how might Mr. Hale have to change in order to understand Minnie Wright the way his wife does?

The relationship between exploratory essays and thesis-driven essays need not be exclusive. If students were to incorporate exploratory writing in the *process* of writing more traditional essays, their disdain for academic writing would diminish, the quality of their writing would improve, and their engagement as writers in school would increase.

Much the same could be said about the research paper with all of the formal requirements and rigid expectations in which it is usually packaged. Is there little wonder that the Courtneys of the world see the research paper as little more than the five-paragraph essay writ longer? As someone who enjoys doing and writing research, I think that's unfortunate because good research is very compatible with exploratory writing.

In exploratory writing, we ask good questions (e.g., Of what value is X? Why does Y even matter? Is it right to Z?); we make careful observations (e.g., of data, historical events, or literature); we wonder what happens when we change something (e.g., a variable or a word in a poem); and we argue for what we think is right (e.g., how to interpret a text, where to invest resources, or how to decide on a case). In research writing, we don't just quote for the sake of quoting; we quote others in order to add integrity and greater worth to our own ideas. We don't just put in facts because teachers expect us to; we find those facts because we *need* them. Clearly, this is not the paradigm of research writing that Courtney has come to know, but it is a time-honored, genuine one nonetheless.

One form this kind of research takes is the I-Search paper, made popular by Ken Macrorie (1988) decades ago. In the I-Search paper, writers search for answers to genuine questions about which they really care. The I-Search paper starts with students' interests and leads them into traditional research databases as well as less traditional ones, such as interviews and self-designed surveys. Here are some sample I-Search questions generated by students in my own composition classes:

- What is the best digital camera to buy for under $300?
- What experimental cancer treatments show promise?
- Why did Thomas Hardy have such a gloomy outlook on life?
- Should I start a Vietnamese restaurant in Denver?
- When do publishers consider a novel good enough to publish it?

Such questions speak to a range of student interests, and their very breadth allows students important choices in what they write about. I-Search papers can facilitate learning in any discipline. In science, for example, students studying toxicology and human health might conduct I-Searches on scientific and ethical issues such as the following:

- How does "secondhand smoke" from a scientist's perspective differ from that of a conscientious expectant mother?
- Why might some people believe, from a scientific viewpoint, that there should be laws banning secondhand smoke in public buildings?
- In a typical day in my life, what natural toxins and which manufactured toxins enter my body? How do they get in? (adapted from American Association for the Advancement of Science's *Science Links*, 2008)

Students who write on topics such as the above must, by necessity, make use of their science knowledge in order to answer their questions, thereby demonstrating their understanding of content as part of the writing process. As you can see in the examples above, it is not difficult for us to help students develop *angles* on subject matter in any content area. In my own classes, I include a lesson on how to develop an interesting angle on a topic (I adapted the lesson from Ballenger, 1993, 2003).

The *journal* goes by many names in school—writer's notebook, learning log, reading log, for example—in addition to journal. Journals allow writers' ideas and language to intersect at the very moment when ideas are created and revised. James Britton (1982) calls this moment "shaping at the point of utterance," or "spontaneous inventiveness," where writing is synonymous with learning in the very act of composing: "Once a writer's words appear on the page," Britton writes, "I believe they act primarily as a stimulus to continuing . . . the movements of the pen capture the movement of our thinking" (pp. 139–140). Learning journals foster engaged writing because writers are free to think through the act of writing, right or wrong and without penalty. Accordingly, exploratory writing in school is

- not graded for correctness or mechanics because writers are free to focus on ideas, not conventions;
- written to record learning, not report learning;
- intended for writers to do something with the subject matter, not merely regurgitate it;
- occasionally skimmed by teachers who assume the role of learning buddy, not evaluator, and who respond to the ideas;
- used before, during, and after reading and class discussion as a way to capture thoughts immediately; and
- kept by teachers also, who show, through modeling, that they too value writing.

TEACHERS RESPOND TO ENGAGED WRITING

We can be a sympathetic audience (a "partner-in-dialogue" Britton, Burgess, Martin, McLeod, & Rosen suggested, 1975), we can downplay mechanics so that we can focus on writers' ideas and stylistic experiments, and we can respond to the writing in timesaving ways. Even with rubrics. If Courtney's teachers were to incorporate learning journals in their classes, they might develop a rubric that not only respects the exploratory nature of writing but also encourages students to take intellectual and stylistic risks. For example, a rubric created specifically for students in an English class included the following criteria:

- In your writing journal, you show how you think about the reading beyond "I like it" or "I didn't like it," as I showed you in class from my own journal.
- You do something with the content of the reading, as I demonstrated in class.
- You take some risks with ideas and with how you write, as you-know-who showed you in class.
- You do some speculating using those familiar stems like "I may be off here, but I think . . ." and "It seems to me that . . ." as my examples in class illustrated.
- When you get stuck, you keep on writing until you get to at least one full page.
- When you have doubts, you state your doubts but try to figure them out. You might say, for example, "I understand _____ but what I don't understand is _____" (Williams, 1990).

- At the end, you look back over what you've written and you say two things you learned that most stand out for you.

With criteria like these, writing journals can be reviewed—for completeness, understanding of content, risk taking, speculation, fluency, and reflection. And the criteria on the rubrics can be tailored for particular assignment—for example, "You show how Hester's character developed in this chapter" or "You show how you can use patterns to communicate ideas in math."

COURTNEY AND SCHOOL WRITING

Engaged writing has the potential to stimulate flow states because, properly executed, it has predictive value:

- *Mind:* It provides a way for students to make meaningful connections; they are the ones making connections through constructive means; they may encounter cognitive dissonance and enjoy the intellectual playfulness needed to work though challenging ideas.
- *Heart:* Engaged writing is mindful writing; it allows writers to focus closely on shaping at the point of utterance in the present; and it provides a safe, semiprivate vehicle for becoming attuned to the self and to others.
- *Flow:* It provides the clear goal of furthering genuine learning; even though writers may not know in advance where the writing will take them, they know it will take them deeper into learning; it provides feedback loops when we respond as sympathetic, interested audiences; and it promotes enjoyment of writing in ways that more rigid forms of school writing usually do not.

In the Introduction to Poetry and Drama class, Courtney kept a reading log, in which she recorded responses to the poems, with particular focus on what she did not understand and how the poem might be considered an expression of human experience (the theme of the course). These informal, first-draft reactions to the readings were shared in class discussions and considered "notes" toward hybrid essays written in the course. Courtney and her peers were encouraged to take risks in their developing understandings by following where ideas led them and by exploring hunches, and they were urged to persevere in writing when faced with difficulties. When research assistants and I read the logs, we viewed the writing in ways similar to what Torbe (1983) calls *enactive writing*—"writing which closely follows the contours of the mind, echoing the processes of understanding at the point of encounter with a text" (p. 164). From this perspective, we observed how students used writing to get below the surface of the poems—we hoped they would move beyond such introductory steps as summarizing the poem, noticing symbols, or saying whether or not they liked it and why. Often writers began with such surface reactions, but then they went further, as we will now see in Courtney's writing.

Writing about Richard Hugo's "Degrees of Gray in Phillipsburg" (see below), she begins by stating that she doesn't like the poem and that she feels she is losing confidence in her ability to make sense of it ("I can't figure out . . ."), but notice how, as she continues to write, she begins to use hypothetical and speculative words ("seems," "I think maybe," and "I would guess") as she keeps at it and nudges her understanding of the poem.

> *I don't really like this poem. I can't figure out what it is saying. The last two lines about the girl's red hair lighting the wall really throws me. I just can't figure out what it means. This poem seems to reveal human experience by comparing one's life to the life of a town. Philipsburg was once a lively and happy town. Now it has died. It is depressing. I think maybe Hugo is trying to say that people go through the same cycle. They live happy lives but in the end they must get old, break down, and die. The speaker of this poem is, I would guess, a man who is realizing that he's getting older. He looks back on the way life used to be and becomes depressed because his life is no longer like this. The setting of this poem is that the speaker is feeling that he is dying with the town. Maybe the last part of the poem is saying that one doesn't have to die with his surroundings. The girl is young and vibrant, indicating perhaps that life goes on. (VanDeWeghe, 1987, p. 45)*

Compare where Courtney began in her response to this poem, from the self-doubt expressed in "The last two lines about the girl's red hair lighting the wall really throws me" to the more confident insights that contradict her opening claim of incompetence—"The girl is young and vibrant, indicating perhaps that life goes on." Do you see how the act of writing has moved her to a place of greater understanding as she wrote her way through doubt and uncertainty? Do you also see how the word *perhaps* signals her continuing sense of tentative exploration?

Responding to Stephen Spender's poem, "I Think Continually of Those Who Were Truly Great," Courtney wrote her way to creating a problem that became more meaningful to her *as she wrote*. Notice how Courtney begins with a half-baked commitment to the assignment ("so that's what

I've come up with"), which, for her, feels like the beginning of closure. But then, at the end of the first paragraph, she discovers a problem, and it troubles her until she writes her way to a hypothetical solution at a crucial eureka moment.

> *"I Think Continually" is beautiful—the images are abstract and fleeting. I've thought for a long time about who "those who were truly great" are. This poem reminds me of an old Catholic hymn about the saints, so that's what I've come up with. Whoever Spender is talking about was barely human—more divine than anything else. I know this because, in the first stanza, the images are like what people who have come back from death describe—tunnels, light, music. In religious tradition, the Holy Spirit is seen as a flame—the people were "touched with fire," and the Spirit was clothed in song. They seem to have been impervious to human desires; desires fell "across their bodies like blossoms"—in other words, gently and driftingly. For most people desires can hit you like a sudden downpour of rain leaving you drenched and surprised and unable to resist. The last word of the second stanza is spirit, but I think this is a different spirit than the "Spirit" of the first stanza.*
>
> *The last stanza describes some more concrete images. It's interesting that the poem proceeds in this manner—Wordsworth, for example, usually described something concrete initially, then went off into the abstract—but that transcendent experience was always anchored in the actual experience. I guess since this poem is not about an actual experience, but rather a collection of experiences and thoughts gleaned from continual musings on "those who were truly great."*
>
> *I can't figure out the second stanza—it may be saying that it is precious never to forget that you are a person—a part of the earth, but that you can't let the world smother your spirit.*
>
> *Oh Wow! "I Think" is about art and artists. That's what Art is about—telling of the Spirit clothed in song, with fire on your lips—yet never forgetting from whence you come. Great Art is often spoken of as a pathway to immortality—to the place where there is no time AND every hour burns bright. (VanDeWeghe, 1987, p. 47)*

One can sense the energy, the voice—the *flow*—in Courtney's final paragraph as she again writes her way to her understanding of the poem. Supporting engaged writers like Courtney is not difficult, nor does it mean we read everything they write: We learn to read selectively and to read quickly. Most important, we learn to read for learning because we read to support learning.

10

Promoting Engagement Through Memory Pathways

In planning the unit on democracy, Ms. Gonzales decided what material would be covered each day for three weeks, what main concepts and their corresponding vocabulary the students needed to learn, and what social studies standards the lesson would address. For her seventh graders, this would be their first encounter with the ideas and terms associated with representative democracy, so the material would be new for virtually all of them. Each day, Ms. Gonzales wrote three key vocabulary words on the board; when students entered the classroom, they knew to write those words in their notebooks because they were told that vocabulary would "show up on the quizzes and final test." Deliberate in her approach to each lesson, Ms. Gonzales paused when one of the vocabulary words came up and directed her students to write in their notebooks, in their own words, what the key terms meant. She spent long stretches of time explaining to her students how the U.S. government works. She often showed diagrams on the overhead projector, such as the timeline and schematic of how a law gets passed. Mostly, she talked or her students read in class, but she always took time to answer questions. Mostly, students listened.

Some days, students read the democracy chapter in their textbook together, in "popcorn" fashion, each student reading aloud to the rest of the class until their teacher said, "Popcorn," at which time the current reader named the next reader, and so on. Other days, the students worked in small groups and read to one another, their reading guide questions at their side since each group was charged with completing answers to the questions by the end of class. As I listened to them read, I thought the text conceptually dense for these students and presented in dry, expository prose (typical of many textbooks). Not surprisingly, the students read in a halting, emotionless fashion, stumbling over or ignoring difficult words to get to the end of their passage. Whenever someone noticed a key vocabulary word, the group stopped their reading and tried to come to consensus on what the vocabulary word meant so they could record in their notebooks the meanings of these terms *in their own words,* as Ms. Gonzales expected.

At the end of the class periods, their teacher talked with students about what they understood from the reading, with particular attention to what students came up with in their definitions of words. Jose, for example, commented that "a branch of the government was like a tree branch that goes out from the tree . . . it's separated but it's still connected." I thought that was a good analogy.

Ms. Gonzales seemed a caring teacher; I especially admired the way she supported the students in finding their own words to explain new vocabulary, and I appreciated the time she took at the end of each class session to review with her students what stood out for them during that class. All in all, she was making worthy attempts to support her students' learning about democracy.

I spoke with Ms. Gonzales when the democracy unit was over and asked her how the students did on the unit review test. She said that the average grade was a C– and that she was disappointed that so many students could not remember the vocabulary words they spent so much time on in class. She said that most of them "got some big ideas like elections and freedom of speech" because they had had experiences with these things at school. But they didn't seem to remember much about the core principles of a democracy, such as states' rights and equal rights, or even the differences between the two houses in Congress. "We covered all those ideas," she complained, "but it was like in one ear and out the other."

I hear the comment about ears a lot from teachers and have even said it myself a few times. The metaphor suggests, visually, that the brain *does* matter when it comes to learning and that students have this remarkable ability to bypass the brain in some baffling anatomical manner whenever they are not engaged. It reminds me of the Genghis Khan story that Csikszentmihalyi (1990b) told when discussing his team's research on what students pay attention to:

In a series of studies teachers were given electronic pagers, and both they and their students were asked to fill out a short questionnaire whenever the pagers signaled (the signal was set to beep at random moments during the fifty-minute periods). In a typical high school history class, the pager went off as the teacher was describing how Genghis Khan had invaded China in 1234. At the same moment, of the twenty-seven students only two were thinking of something even remotely related to China. One of these two students was remembering a dinner she had had recently with her family at a Chinese restaurant; the other was wondering why Chinese men used to wear their hair in ponytails. (p. 134)

What's going on here—and in other classrooms where teachers talk *at* students the majority of the time? For one, these teachers believe that the business of schooling is the transfer of knowledge from teachers' minds or from books to students' minds. It is not my intent here to enter into criticism of the transmission view of learning, except to say that when we teach by saying things to students *that we wish them to remember,* as in giving lectures or providing instructions, we really believe that they will remember what we say, or at least the gist of what we say. For another, we expect that they can use their semantic pathways (word paths) to memory—and that they will store in long-term memory information we endeavor to cover in our curricula. Yet, as every teacher knows, to his or her frustration, too often "it goes in one ear and out the other." Oddly, that same teacher persists in teaching as if students *will* remember—in spite of evidence to the contrary—that somehow they might become engaged just by listening most of their day. Memory and engagement do go hand in hand, as Willis (2006*) reminds us: "When brain research on memory and retention is applied to the classroom, it not only drives the learning process, but it also allows educators to energize and enliven the minds of their students" (p. 36). But there is not just one pathway—listening—for remembering.

MEMORY PATHWAYS

Semantic Pathways

The *semantic memory pathway* transmits linguistic information through auditory and printed language, most commonly in the forms of discussion, lectures, and textbooks. School increasingly favors auditory and visual-verbal learners because instruction through listening and reading increases as students progress through the grades. From the brain's perspective, however, the semantic pathway to remembering is the least efficient way of getting information into *long-term memory* where it can be stored and retrieved with the right retrieval strategies. Researchers believe that our *short-term memory* can store information for up to 30 seconds, after which time it's either used (e.g., rehearsed through repetition) or it's lost. Another kind of memory, *working memory,* can hold limited amounts of information for hours, as when students cram for exams the night before. Semantic information (oral or written words) must be repeated or meaningfully linked to existing knowledge in order to make it into long-term memory. If it isn't linked to existing knowledge, it's meaningless; if it isn't ingrained into the pathway through, say, association, repetition, or mnemonics, then it's not going to stick.

You can see the problem: Students are expected to use their semantic pathways to learn throughout the bulk of their schooling, yet the time limitations in short-term memory (5–30 seconds) and the storage limitations in working memory (7 +/− 2 chunks of information) make semantic pathways the most inefficient way to remember. Talking may be the easiest way to teach, but for many, listening is certainly not the easiest way to learn. Although some students are better at listening than others, and although some topics garner more attention than others, the fact remains that other memory pathways need to be used more if we are to help students remember more.

So why does such an overreliance on semantic memory persevere in schools? One reason is that many believe the myth that telling *is* teaching. Most teachers were taught this way, and, commonly, they teach the way they were taught. Another is that many teachers believe that demands to cover the curriculum mandate the most time-efficient ways of helping students learn. Unfortunately, efficiency of time does not equate to amount of learning since there are real limits to what brains can process in time, not to mention all those other things that detour our attention, such as that Chinese dinner enjoyed just last night!

A third reason is that many teachers teach the way they believe *they* learn best, and that is through language. Teacher education programs (higher education is biased toward semantic learning) provide the training ground for instructional practices, and their own mode of operation is primarily through semantic memory pathways.

Episodic Pathways

Episodic pathways make use of physical locations, events, or lived or imagined experiences situated in place and time. Dramatically narrated historical events and stories are the stuff of episodic pathways. So are creative dramatics and films. When we introduce a novel by first telling students how the protagonist's problem in the story came about, we appeal to episodic memory pathways. When we interrupt a lecture to tell an illustrative anecdote, we do so because we hope students will connect the semantic content of the lecture with the episodic pathway triggered by the anecdote. Crafted narratives illuminate expository material in any subject area; whether such stories are "true" or not is less important than what they do for supporting learners' memory, as you may recall from the story John told in that statistics class (see Preface). Barell (1995) points the way for us to use the power of episodic memory pathways when he writes,

> All subjects have within them stories, since these subjects or areas of inquiry are human creations. The humanities, mathematics, sciences, and the practical and performing arts are ways we humans have of investigating the world and the universe, ways of searching for and fashioning meaning. . . .
>
> Thus, our curriculum is composed of subjects, each of which is a story of doubt and uncertainty resolved by many people on a quest for understanding . . . To treat these stories as bundles of dissociated facts is to shred these gripping dramas into isolated scenes and monologues, signifying very little. (p. 132)

For us, the trick, if there is any, is to figure out how to integrate narratives that illuminate and support the expository "material" of curriculum.

Procedural Pathways

Procedural memory pathways make use of the body in motion, or kinesthetic movement—lab experiments being the most familiar in schools. Procedural memory also comes into play for practical activities such as tying a knot and booting up a computer. In English, some teachers have procedures for studying literature (e.g., literature circles) that use set roles and routines for when students work in small groups; these too rely on procedural memory. Some teachers have students move around the physical space of the classroom as a way of supporting procedural memory. In her book on learning and memory, Sprenger (1999) recommends

> anything that provides movement—for example, role-playing, debate, dance, marches, monologues, and games. Making shadow boxes can enhance procedural memory. Sock-puppet shows can reinforce many concepts in any content area. These procedures not only reinforce semantic knowledge, but they also represent memories that can be stored through those procedural memory

"muscles." If you have trouble applying your content to any of these, use your imagination. Have students stand up as you cover specific material. Ask them to walk as you review it, jump when they think they understand a particular point, and clap when they know it all. All of that movement and fun will make a big impression on their brains. (p. 74)

Emotional Pathways

Some researchers believe that *emotional memory pathways* draw on what Pert (1997) calls the "molecules of emotion" to facilitate memory. While both negative and positive emotions impact this pathway, we know that negative ones may cause the brain to downshift, while positive ones will bolster the brain's neurotransmitters' ability to enhance long-term memory through chemical stimulation. Some consider emotional memory pathways to be the most powerful because these chemical reactions create a stronger imprint in long-term memory. Music, dramatic tension, celebration, laughter, passion for content—such are some of the ways we can boost the power of emotional memory pathways. So-called inspirational speakers often work the emotional memory pathways when appealing to their audiences. It is interesting, also, how craftily people running for public office appeal to emotional pathways when they claim to identify with their constituents' struggles, tell the stories of their own struggles, or attack their opponents. I make this observation not as a criticism but as an insight into how we could rely more on emotional pathways to engage students in their subject matter.

Spatial Pathways

Spatial memory pathways rely on visual or graphic representations to get information into long-term memory—maps, diagrams, pictures, and graphs are the most common ones in schools. Some students seem to be more oriented toward spatial pathways than other types, so that, for them, a picture literally *is* worth a thousand words. Ask them to verbalize the setting in a story, and they go blank, but ask them to draw it, and they can easily recall dimensions and details. *Spatial learners*, students with strong spatial memory pathways, attune themselves to information that is primarily nonverbal. Florey (2005) describes how the linear dimensions of diagramming sentences supported her spatial memory pathway in learning sentence structure in school:

I learned it in sixth grade from Sister Bernadette. I can still see her: a tiny nun with a sharp pink nose, confidently drawing a dead-straight horizontal line like a highway across the blackboard, flourishing her chalk in the air at the end of it, her veil flapping out behind her as she turned back to the class. "We begin," she said, "with a straight line." And then, in her firm and saintly script, she put words on the line, a noun and a verb—probably something like *dog barked.* Between the lines she drew a short vertical slash, bisecting the line. Then she made a road that forked off at an angle—a short country lane under the word *dog*—and on it she wrote *The.* . . .

That was it: subject, predicate, and the little modifying article that civilized the sentence—all of it made into a picture that was every bit as clear and informative as an actual portrait of a beagle in mid-woof. The thrilling part was that this was a picture not of the animal but of the words that stood for the animal and its noises. It was a representation of something both concrete and abstract. The diagram was a bit like art, a bit like mathematics. It was much more than words uttered or words written: it was a picture of language. (p. 32)

While I doubt that Florey's (2005) nostalgic admiration for sentence diagramming will hasten its return to most schools, her description does show us how the visual aspects support the verbal ones, and it suggests that we should think more about how the interplay of verbal and visual information can support multiple memory pathways in learning anything.

MULTIPLE MEMORY PATHWAYS

With multiple pathways, brains access and store information in combinations of semantic, episodic, procedural, emotional, and spatial ways. If we realize that students, like all people, have multiple memory pathways, some more accessible than others, then we ought to gear instruction toward as many pathways as possible. Sprenger (1999) reminds us that the "more memory lanes you can reach and teach to, the more successful your students will be in their learning" (p. 76). She recommends a memory-based way of thinking about lesson planning that uses multiple memory "lanes":

- As you plan a unit of instruction, evaluate how much of the material is aimed at the semantic lane. Are there ways you can teach that information through the other lanes?
- Next, decide how you can create an environment that will engage the episodic memory.

- Analyze the material to determine which procedures are built in, or which ones you need to create.
- Can you make this material emotional? Are there popular songs that might be associated with this material? Ask the students what they know about this new information. This may add to their feelings about it.

A middle school teacher and staff developer, Sprenger (1999) notes the relationship between teaching for multiple memory pathways and student engagement when she describes her unit on teaching Gary Paulsen's novel, *The Rifle:*

> I had to use conscious effort to access all of those memory lanes. The unit became more interesting as I did so. The students were involved and happy. Each year I must add some units and change others to access all of the memory lanes. It can be a challenge, but the rewards are worth it. (p. 79)

Remembering through multiple pathways is natural because it more closely approximates life outside of school, where students have opportunity to learn voluntarily, and where they do not have to rely on semantic memory pathways alone to process and store information. If we want to predict engagement by planning geared toward multiple memory pathways, the following predictability issues may be addressed:

- *Mind:* Students' brains will be able to make connections through a variety of pathways (e.g., semantic, spatial, episodic, etc.) rather than through just one (e.g., semantic).
- *Heart:* Because mindfulness depends on the brain's ability to pay attention, multiple rather than single ways of getting information into and out of long-term memory enhance learning.
- *Flow:* Because there are biological limits to the amount of information brains can process through semantic pathways (semantic bottlenecks), students are better able to concentrate on learning through many pathways.

ENGAGED REMEMBERING IN MS. GONZALES'S CLASSROOM

So what can Ms. Gonzales do to better support her students' memory work in the democracy unit? If she were to have followed the advice suggested by Sprenger (1995, 2005), here is how she might have described her thinking for the democracy unit.

In preparing the unit, I notice that all of the information on democracy will be presented in the textbook and supplemented by my own class comments on the reading. For this unit, I always have my students read a handout article on how the three branches of government interact on a sample piece of legislation. Other than a few visuals in the textbook, everything will be processed through semantic pathways. That has to change. I'm thinking that I need to present some of the information in narratives so that the episodic memory pathways will be addressed. I'll also need to get physical movement going—perhaps dramatize the three branches of government interaction through groups in the room or organize a field trip to the capitol. We can have the groups work on procedural and spatial memory pathways by charting out how a law gets made, maybe one that bears on students' lives to arouse their emotional memory pathways, like making school not mandatory before age 16, or censoring music videos.

I can support episodic memory pathways by getting some adolescent literature with democracy themes from the library and asking the school librarian to hold book talks on them for my students. Then I can offer extra credit for anyone who reads a story about democracy. I can also invite students to write stories about some of the topics in the unit, like what might happen if a tyrant in the Executive Branch abused the balance of power principle, or how a group of students create their own democracy in their own school for the future. I can also tell stories that illustrate some of the major decisions handed down by the Supreme Court, like Brown v. Board of Education. *I can even tell about my own experiences in growing up and how they reflect the principles of democracy, like how my large family of seven used to decide on vacations or how we made the "rules of the house" so that my brothers and sisters could learn to get along.*

Even though the study of democracy seems dry, it should be easy to put some emotion into it in other ways too. We can use debates on the civil rights legislation and role-playing about declarations of war to get the emotions excited. If we do some role-playing about declarations of war, I might show some war photos or read some narratives about war from soldiers' perspectives or the perspectives of civilians. I'll need to remember to check often how students are feeling about some of the issues we study, and remember to celebrate their explorations and discoveries a lot too.

For these multiple memory pathway ideas, all of the principles of democracy are in the textbook, but so are some of the procedures, like how a law gets passed. The problem is that the procedures are just explained in words, and what I need to do is to figure out how to get the students to experience the procedures physically. I suppose that I could have student research teams do Internet searches for other procedures and then they could present their research in some kinesthetic ways to the rest of the class. Role-playing would also be an option, like creating Congressional speeches in favor of and opposed to legislation; I could show some C-SPAN clips to help students learn how lawmakers give speeches.

Now integrating multiple memory pathways into her instructional planning, Ms. Gonzales also begins to help students learn *strategies* for remembering. Perhaps she takes time during class for students to *rehearse* memory material—again, using multiple pathways such as pair sharing or role-playing. Perhaps she asks students to represent their understandings of concepts by creating visual tools that re-present verbal information in graphic ways (see Burke, 2002, for ideas on graphic ways to present information). (Higbee, 2001, and Sprenger, 2005, have many excellent ideas on how to help students remember).

Afterword

Lingering Questions

This book began as an inquiry into engagement that was driven by questions. I'd always known that asking "Does X work?" in the classroom was important. In this inquiry, however, *what* and *how* questions became more important:

- What makes students excited about learning, and conversely, what makes them disaffected or only marginally involved?
- What do flow experiences have to teach us about the nature of engaged learning?
- How can we plan our teaching based on a deep understanding of student minds and hearts when they're truly engaged in learning?
- What do typical classroom activities such as reading and discussing look like when they are guided by mind- and heart-based engagement theory?

Taking the perspective that engaged learning approximates flow states (Chapter 1) led to thinking of flow as having a neurological component (mind based—Chapter 2) and a humanistic component (heart based—Chapter 3). When these two dimensions are combined and used as a lens through which we think about teaching and learning, we develop *wholesight*, as we view instructional practice as engaging both the brains and the hearts of learners. Applying wholesight during instructional planning (Chapter 4) helps us be more deliberate in planning *for* engagement based on what we anticipate will be the mind-, heart-, and flow-based experiences of learners in our classrooms. In more typical planning, we determine the content to be covered, draw on certain practices to get the content "across," and then decide on a method to assess student knowledge or performance at some point. With wholesight planning, content coverage is still determined and potential activities still considered, but through the wholesight lens, we ask key questions (Chapter 4) about how those activities are more or less likely to engage students in the learning, especially as we come to know our students more.

We then considered an array of typical classroom activities—modeling, talking, reading, and so on—and examined each from the engagement perspective in order to show how instructional practice can be revised to bring about greater engagement among learners of all ages and in all subjects. It is my hope that some headway has been made here toward understanding what makes students excited about learning, as well as toward understanding how flow helps us promote engaged learning and how we can plan instruction toward that end through some specific engaging instructional practices that are also supported by empirical research.

I have lingering questions, however, about integrating the classroom practices presented chapter by chapter in Part II. Wholesight planning for classroom practice necessarily integrates these activities. How can we, for instance, not think about *talking* if we intend to model literacy practices for our students? Is it even possible to consider *reading* without considering *memory pathways?* And so I wonder, if we *do* separate engaged learning activities in classroom practice, how does that affect student learning and achievement?

There is a tension here between trying to do everything we can at once (e.g., model work habits, support reading instruction, write to learn) to engage learners and finding the time to do one thing pretty well before adding more complexity. How can we find the time to fully and thoughtfully integrate our own understanding of engaged teaching with instructional planning? Most of us have hardly enough time for planning in our daily "plan" period relative to all the diverse students we teach, the number of classes for which we are responsible, and the many interruptions and meetings that find their way into our days. In Chapter 4, I recommended that we build, over time, greater familiarity with holistic engagement by applying the questions selectively—because wholesight is a way of thinking about planning instructional practices. As we integrate the classroom activities discussed in Part II into our existing approaches, we might go slowly, noting the effects over time. For instance, perhaps we just focus on engaged reading for a while and then integrate writing, followed by modeling, and so on, one layer informing another—as wholesight builds.

Still other questions linger.

WHAT ABOUT ASSESSMENT?

The current state of empirical research on engagement presents strong evidence that the greater the levels of engagement, the greater the impact:

> Engagement is associated with positive academic outcomes, including achievement and persistence in school; and it is higher in classrooms with supportive teachers and peers, challenging and authentic tasks, opportunities for choice, and sufficient structure. (Fredericks et al., 2004, p. 87)

This should surprise no one, and it should give us much confidence with its global confirmation of the value of engagement as an instructional goal. Our problem, however, is how we can know if our instructional practices make a difference in our own classrooms, which is an assessment issue at the local level. We must begin with pre-assessing students' knowledge about a topic as well as their academic abilities. These data become our baseline for working with individual students and for differentiating instruction. Comprehensive assessment of this sort, though critical, is beyond my scope here, though many good resources are available and accessible (see, for example, Hubbard & Power, 2003; Kuhs, Johnson, Agruso, & Monrad, 2001; Shea, Murray, & Harlin, 2005)

Nonetheless, how *can* we know if our teaching practices based on wholesight work with *our* students—for example, to increase motivation, to create greater involvement, and to increase achievement? In some ways the assessment question is a difficult one to answer because engagement is not easily assessed. We can't go inside the brain to check on the amount of neurological activity, the way a researcher would, through such technology as functional magnetic resonance imaging (fMRI). Nor can we somehow measure heart-based engagement through technological means—not yet, at any rate. This is not to say, however, that engagement cannot be assessed, for we can determine the effectiveness of engaging teaching practices in a number of familiar, acceptable ways.

One way is for us to become mindful in the classroom, *noticing and observing visual and behavioral signs* of engaged learning, such as the following:

- Students are reluctant to stop a learning activity.
- Their behaviors take on an energetic edge, such as increased on-task talk with others.
- They ask for more of the activity, such as more math problems or more time to read and write. Similarly, they reveal interest in exploring individual projects.

- Distractions, such as ambient noise in the classroom, do not deter them from the learning. Conversely, they complain about distractions.
- Students notice that their peers are becoming more enthusiastic and involved.
- They concentrate on the task, or they are able to sustain with greater independence.
- Behavioral problems diminish or disappear.
- Their involvement in the community of learners deepens. For instance, they show greater ability to lead and follow, collaborate with others, try out new skills, and personalize assignments. Some just begin doing homework!

In addition to observing the behavioral signs of engagement, we can also *listen carefully to what students say.* One college composition student, for example, wrote an argumentative essay on the Arab-Israeli conflict that had two sides, one of which she fervently believed to be right (she was of Palestinian descent), and the other wrong. After examining sides of the issue other than her own *with compassion,* she said that she had "changed her mind" and wanted to qualify her argumentative thesis to show that there was validity on both sides of the conflict. I see that changed mind as a signal that she was engaged in her research and writing.

As another example, a middle school student was thoroughly engaged in writing an original one-act play; in a conference with her teacher, she said, "I *really really* want to finish writing the play so that I can get my friends to perform it for the class." The emotional imperative in her words stands as a clear sign of engagement as we understand it now.

Along with noticing what students tell us, we can *ask students directly to describe their engagement* through such means as written reflections, self reports, drawings, checklists, attitude inventories, rating scales, and questionnaires. (For a good summary of such assessment tools, see "Assessing Student Engagement Rates" in ERIC Clearinghouse, 2005.)

Finally, engagement can be assessed through the *products* of student achievement—such as written journals, tests, papers, and dramatic performances. For example, in a writing class, we could ask students to add an *epilogue* to their essays in which they discuss when, if at all, during the writing of the essay they felt engaged with the subject. Or in social studies, math, or science, students can write reflections on their experience with a learning activity. In the case of such written products, the prompts for the writing must be designed to elicit reflection upon engagement. Here is an example from a history class.

You have just completed the unit on the American Revolution. During this time, we as a class have had many experiences with this important time in our nation's history. We have read in the textbook and in other source materials, researched on the Internet, held small-group discussions, and wrote stories as if we were actually alive during that time. Please spend a little time writing a letter to me about what you feel was the most engaging part for you during this unit. Please be specific. This will have no bearing on your grade; it's just for me to learn more about you as a learner.

Once we begin collecting data on student engagement in these ways, we become, by default, teacher-researchers as our students, through the assessment data they provide, teach *us* about engaged learning.

WHAT ABOUT CLASSROOM RESEARCH?

When we collect data on achievement and become teacher-researchers, our classrooms become sites of inquiry as we learn more about engaged learning. Our students provide vital data for us as we look for the physical/social signs of engagement, listen as they describe engagement, and invite them to report about their engagement. Through this data, we confirm or disconfirm the effectiveness of teaching practices. We empower ourselves when we have data in hand, in effect saying, "Here is how I taught X, and here is how I *know* it worked." This is the kind of data-driven instruction that empowers us as teachers.

Through such assessment, we can learn where students were more—or less—engaged, and we can revise instructional practices as we aim for greater engagement. At the same time, however, we must ask, What is the impact on student *learning?* Although students may be highly engaged in a classroom activity, how do we know if academic achievement is affected? To answer the achievement question, teacher-researchers can gather their own data on student achievement through many of the same standard-assessment measures used to assess engagement itself:

- Student work samples (e.g., writing, projects exhibitions, performances)
- Portfolios of student work over time
- Standardized achievement measures
- Regular classroom tests and quizzes
- Anecdotal records
- Recording of class discussions
- Responses to a class blog
- Individual conferences
- Student attendance and behavior records

- Surveys, inventories, checklists
- Self-evaluations and course evaluations

Classroom inquiry starts with good questions about learners. It may or may not lead to answers because its primary goal is insight and understanding. If answers are found, they may not be easy answers, and they may open up other lines of investigation. Inquiry into engagement is no different from other kinds of teacher research in that the questions asked are much the same—how, what, and why questions probe and penetrate, as Hubbard and Power (1999) remind us,

> The best research questions often begin with the words *what* or *how*. *Why* questions ask you to trace the source of a phenomenon. You can develop a hypothesis as to why something occurs, but to conclusively identify the source is virtually impossible. By contrast, *what* and *how* questions lead you toward descriptions of phenomena. (p. 33)

Teacher-research questions originate in a particular setting with particular students and demographic context. Here are the types of questions teacher-researchers may want to ask as they explore lines of inquiry into engaged learning:

- What happens in my class discussion when the entire group seems engaged? What precipitates such moments? Who's doing most of the talking and questioning? Why does the discussion die down after a while?
- What kinds of questions do students ask when they see me demonstrate my reading strategies for challenging texts?
- Are there differences in student writing when they write to prove learning compared to when they write to learn? If so, what are those differences?
- How do my students talk about intelligence? Do I notice any changes once I begin using words that support engaged learning?
- How do my students describe how they remember school content? What memory pathways do they seem to be using most of the time? What happens to their ability to remember if I teach them alternative memory pathways? Which pathways work better with some students than with others?
- As I model habits of mind and heart, what evidence might I notice that my students are taking on those habits? What evidence do I actually see or hear?

- How might wholesight planning affect special populations of students, such as English language learners, twice exceptional students, or students with learning disabilities?

Conducting classroom inquiry gives us solid research-based foundations for making wise instructional decisions and explaining (if not defending) those decisions. When we add data derived from our assessment of engaged learners and when we incorporate instructional practices that have a proven impact on achievement, we give an empirical dimension to our instructional practice, one that adds integrity to our reflective practice.

WHAT ABOUT STUDY GROUPS?

I've found that collaborating with other teachers is more interesting and more supportive than working alone, and it generates more learning in a shorter time. That's why I think the engaged learning perspective put forth here is suitable for school-based study groups or similar professional learning communities where we can ask important questions about engagement in diverse school settings, share with other teachers what we learn from classroom experiments, collectively examine student work samples for the impact on achievement, and ask critical "So what?" questions.

Effective study groups involve a group of teachers (often administrators too) who regularly meet face-to-face and/or electronically to investigate a topic of common interest, to develop expertise about an issue critical to their school or department, or to collaborate on classroom research. They read common materials, discuss their learning as critical friends would, apply what they learn to their work with students, gather data, share the data with one another, and, through the entire process, form a dynamic professional-development force (and agent for change) in their department, school, or district.

Study groups and similar professional learning communities incorporate many of the best aspects of professional development. Guskey (2003), for example, in "What Makes Professional Development Effective?" cites six ways in which study groups nurture and develop teacher knowledge and expertise:

- Enhance teachers' understanding of teaching and learning
- Provide opportunity for collaboration and collegial exchange
- Promote genuine inquiry into schoolwide issues
- Foster data collection to enhance understanding and guide practices
- Value site-based knowledge and experience
- Develop [leadership within] a learning community

Were you to use this book as a basis for study groups, you could proceed in a number of ways. One way would be to read Part I for understanding and clarity in order to "get" the main ideas and check your evolving understanding against one another's; then move on to Part II, chapter by chapter, each time considering how the practices described there support or challenge prevailing instructional practices.

Another approach would be to start with the chapters in Part II, experiment with those classroom activities with your own students, and collect data to bring back to the group to share and compare with colleagues. At the same time, you would read the first part of the book and discuss how Part I illuminates Part II.

These are just two possible ways to proceed; I'm sure you and your colleagues can think of others. I'm partial to the first one because Part I lays the intellectual foundation for Part II, and that's the order my mind generally prefers. Part II, on the other hand, offers more concrete activities that will generate classroom data, and that's very engaging work too, especially for those of you who want to dig right in with instructional practices.

If you are interested in starting a study group, I would recommend a few sources that provide diverse models as well as tips on how study groups work well. One is the Web site of the National Writing Project (www.writing project.org), where you'll find examples of study groups embedded in schools that exemplify the principles of effective professional development Guskey (2003) and others (Chappuis, Chappuis, & Stiggins 2009; Darling-Hammond & Richardson, 2009) write about. Key in *study groups* and you'll find many resources, including the ones I worked with in the Denver Writing Project. Another great source for getting a study group off and running would be *Teacher Study Groups*, by Birchak et al., (1998). This book lays out many useful tips and procedures for launching study groups and, most important, for providing the leadership that makes them successful.

WHAT NOW?

Today my Google search with the key words *engagement & learning* turned up 24,400,000 entries. After reviewing a number of entries, I was reminded just how many people other than you and me want to increase student engagement and how many have suggestions on how to do that. These ideas range widely, and most should be familiar to anyone who cares about education. Here are a few:

- Develop and enforce academic standards.
- Decrease school size.
- Develop personal relationships with students.

- Use culturally sensitive classroom materials.
- Eliminate tracking.
- Pay students.
- Enforce academic rigor.
- Lengthen the school day.
- Better prepare teachers.
- Ensure teacher subject knowledge.
- Teach to the developmental needs of students.
- Have coherent curriculum.
- Ensure safe schools.

This is just the start of what is likely a very long list of methods to increase engagement in learning, and I'm sure you have your suggestions too. In this book, I've set forth my ideas on the natural ways that the minds and hearts of learners get engaged. Engaged learning, I've said, ought to go *with* nature, not *against* nature. The more school resembles the natural ways students learn anything, anywhere, the more likely students will learn and achieve in ways that astonish their teachers, parents, friends, and even themselves. We ought to align ourselves and our instructional practices with nature so that school becomes less unnatural and more meaningful and so that students use their minds and hearts so that learning becomes truly compelling.

References

Alliance for Excellent Education. (2004). *Reading next* (2nd ed.). New York: Carnegie Corporation.

Ambrose, J. (1987). Music journals. In T. Fulwiler. (Ed.), *The journal book* (pp. 261–268). Portsmouth, NH: Boynton Cook.

American Association for the Advancement of Science. (2008). *Science links.* Retrieved April 16, 2008, from www.sciencenetlinks.com/lessons.cfm?Grade=912&BenchmarkID=6&DocID=431

Angier, N. (2007). *The canon.* Boston: Houghton Mifflin.

Ballenger, B. (1993). Teaching the research paper. In T. Newkirk (Ed.), *Nuts and bolts: A practical guide to teaching college composition* (pp. 129–150). Portsmouth, NH: Heinemann.

Ballenger, B. (2003). *The curious researcher: A guide to writing research papers* (4th ed.). New York: Longman.

Barell, J. (1995). *Teaching for thoughtfulness* (2nd ed.). White Plains, NY: Longman.

Barell, J. (2003). *Developing more curious minds.* Alexandria, VA: Association for Supervision and Curriculum Development.

Benjamin, A. (2007). *But I'm not a reading teacher: Strategies for literacy instruction in the content areas.* Larchmont, NY: Eye on Education.

Berninger, V. W., & Richards, T. L. (2002). *Brain literacy for educators and psychologists.* San Diego, CA: Academic Press.

Biancarosa, G. (2005). After third grade. *Educational Leadership, 63*(2), 16–22.

Birchak, B., Connor, D., Crawford, K. M., Kahn, L., Kaser, S., Turner, S., et al. (1998). *Teacher study groups.* Urbana, IL: National Council of Teachers of English.

Blau, S. (2003). *The literature workshop: Teaching texts and their readers.* Portsmouth, NH: Heinemann.

Britton, J. (1982). Shaping at the point of utterance. In G. M. Pradl (Ed.), *Prospect and retrospect* (pp. 139–145). Portsmouth, NH: Boynton/Cook.

Britton, J., Burgess, T., Martin, N., McLeod, A., & Rosen, H. (1975). *The development of writing abilities (11–18).* London: Schools Council Project.

Brooks, J. G. (2004). To see beyond the lesson. *Educational Leadership, 62*(1), 8–12.

Brooks, J. G., & Brooks, M. G. (1999). *In search of understanding: The case for constructivist classrooms.* Alexandria, VA: Association for Supervision and Curriculum Development.

Bruner, J. (1986). *Actual minds, possible worlds.* Cambridge, MA: Harvard University Press.

Burke, J. (2002). *Tools for thought.* Portsmouth, NH: Heinemann.

Caine, R. N., & Caine, G. (1994). *Making connections: Teaching and the human brain.* Alexandria, VA: Association for Supervision and Curriculum Development.

Caine, R. N., & Caine, G. (1997). *Education on the edge of possibility.* Alexandria, VA: Association for Supervision and Curriculum Development.

Caine, R. N., & Caine, G. (2001). *The brain, education, and the competitive edge.* Alexandria, VA: Association for Supervision and Curriculum Development.

Caplan, R., & Keech, C. (1990). *Showing writing: A training program to help students be specific.* Berkeley, CA: Bay Area Writing Project.

Chappuis, S., Chappuis, J., & Stiggins, R. (2009). Supporting teacher learning teams. *Educational Leadership, 66*(5), 55–60.

Chiarella, T. (2004). The $20 theory of the universe. In S. Orlean (Ed.), *The best American magazine writing 2004* (pp. 410–421). New York: Harper Collins.

Churchland, P. S. (2004). How do neurons know? *Daedalus, 142*(2), 42–50.

Costa, A. L. (Ed.). (2001). *Developing minds: A resource book for teaching thinking* (3rd ed.). Alexandria, VA: Association for Supervision and Curriculum Development.

Cotton, K. (1988). *Classroom questioning.* Retrieved May 21, 2008, from the Northwest Regional Educational Library Web site at www.nwrel.org/scpd/sirs/3/cu5.html

Csikszentmihalyi, M. (1990a). *Flow: The psychology of optimal experience.* New York: Harper & Row.

Csikszentmihalyi, M. (1990b). Literacy and intrinsic motivation. *Daedalus, 119*(2), 115–142.

Csikszentmihalyi, M. (1997). *Finding flow: The psychology of engagement with everyday life.* New York: Basic Books.

Csikszentmihalyi, M., Rathunde, K., Whalen, S., & Wong, M. (1993). *Talented teenagers: The roots of success & failure.* Cambridge, MA: Cambridge University Press.

Darling-Hammond, L. & Richardson, N. (2009). Teacher learning: What matters? *Educational Leadership 66*(5), 46–53.

Drapeau, P. (2008). *Differentiating with graphic organizers.* Thousand Oaks, CA: Corwin.

Dweck, C. S. (2002). Messages that motivate: How praise molds students' beliefs, motivation, and performance (in surprising ways). In J. Aronson (Ed.), *Improving academic achievement* (pp. 37–60). London: Academic Press.

Dweck, C. S. (2006). *Mindset.* New York: Random House.

Egan, K. (1997). *The educated mind: How cognitive tools shape our understanding.* Chicago: University of Chicago Press.

Elbow, P. (1981). *Writing with power.* New York: Oxford University Press.

Engagement. (1989). *In Oxford English Dictionary.* Retrieved October 19, 2005, from www.dictionary.oed.com

ERIC Clearinghouse. (2005). Assessing student engagement rates. *ERIC Digest.* Retrieved October 19, 2005, from www.ericdigest.org/2005–2/engagement.html

Florey, K. B. (2005). Sister Bernadette's barking dog. In S. Orlean (Ed.), *The best American essays 2005* (pp. 31–36). New York: Houghton Mifflin

Fredericks, J. A., Blumenfeld, P. S., & Paris, A. H. (2004). School engagement: Potential of the concept, state of the evidence. *Review of Educational Research 74*, 59–98.

Gardener, H. (1991). *The unschooled mind.* New York: Basic Books.

Garner, B. K. (2008). When students seem stalled. *Educational Leadership 65*(6), 32–38.

Glazer, S. (Ed.), (1999). *The heart of learning: Spirituality in education.* New York: Penguin Putnam.

Goldberg, N. (2000). *Thunder and lightning.* New York: Bantam Books.

Goleman, D. (1995). *Emotional intelligence.* New York: Bantam Books.

Graves, D. H. (1983). *Writing: Teachers & children at work.* Portsmouth, NH: Heinemann.

Gurian, M., Henley, P., & Trueman, T. (2001). *Boys and girls learn differently! A guide for teachers and parents.* San Francisco: Jossey-Bass.

Gurian, M., & Stevens, K. (2004). With boys and girls in mind. *Educational Leadership, 62*(3), 21–26.

Guskey, T. (2003). What makes professional development effective? *Phi Delta Kappan, 84*(10), 748–750.

Hahn, T. N. (1998). *The heart of the Buddha's teaching.* Berkeley, CA: Parallax Press.

Hashimoto, I. Y. (1991). *Thirteen weeks.* Portsmouth, NH: Heinemann.

Higbee, K. (2001). *Your memory: How it works and how to improve it.* Cambridge, MA: DeCapo Press.

Higginson, T. W. (1891). *Emily Dickinson's letters.* Retrieved May 7, 2008, from www.earlywomenmasters.net/essays/authors/higginson/twh_dickinson.html

Hill, J. D., & Flynn, K. M. (2006). *Classroom instruction that works with English language learners.* Alexandria, VA: Association for Supervision and Curriculum Development.

Hubbard, R. H., & Power, B. M. (1999). *Living the questions.* York, ME: Stenhouse.

Hubbard, R. H., & Power, B. M. (2003). *The art of classroom inquiry.* Portsmouth, NH: Heinemann.

Hyerle, D. (2008). *Visual tools for transforming information into knowledge.* Thousand Oaks, CA: Corwin.

International Reading Association. (2002). *Summary of the (U.S.) national reading panel report: Teaching children to read.* Newark, DE: International Reading Association.

Jensen, E. (1998). *Teaching with the brain in mind.* Alexandria, VA: Association for Supervision and Curriculum Development.

Johnston, M. (2003). *In the deep heart's core.* New York: Grove Press.

Johnston, P. H. (2004). *Choice words: How our language affects children's learning.* Portland, ME: Stenhouse.

Keene, E. (2008). *To understand.* Portsmouth, NH: Heinemann.

Kessler, R. (1999). Nourishing students in secular schools. *Educational Leadership, 56*(4), 49–52.

Kohn, A. (2004). Challenging students—and how to have more of them. *Phi Delta Kappan, 86*(3), 184–194.

Kozol, J. (2005, September). Still separate, still unequal: America's educational apartheid. *Harper's Magazine,* 41–54.

Kuhs, T. M., Johnson, R. L., Agruso, S. A., & Monrad, D. M. (2001). *Put to the test.* Portsmouth, NH: Heinemann.

Langer, J. A. (2002). *Effective literacy instruction: Building successful reading and writing programs.* Urbana, IL: National Council of Teachers of English.

Lappan, G., Fey, J. T., Fitzgerald, W. M., Friel, S. N., & Phillips, E. D. (2004). *Connected Mathematics: Moving straight ahead.* Needham, MA: Pearson.

LeDoux, J. (1996). *The emotional brain.* New York: Simon & Schuster.

The Literacy Web. (2008). *Content area literacy.* Retrieved March 18, 2008, from www.literacy.uconn.edu/contlit.htm

Lyons, C. (2003). *Teaching struggling readers: How to use brain-based research to maximize learning.* Portsmouth, NH: Heinemann.

Macrorie, K. (1988). *The I-search paper.* Portsmouth, NH: Heinemann.

Martin, N., D'Arcy, P., Newton, B., & Parker, R. (1976). *Writing and learning across the curriculum 11–16.* London: Schools Council Publication.

Marzano, R., Pickering, D. J., & Pollock, J. E. (2001). *Classroom instruction that works: Research-based strategies for increasing student achievement.* Alexandria, VA: Association for Supervision and Curriculum Development.

Mehan, H. (1979). What time is it, Denise? Asking known-information questions in classroom practice. *Theory Into Practice, 18*(4), 285–294.

Moffett, J. (1994). *The universal schoolhouse: Spiritual awakening through education.* Portland, ME: Calendar Island.

Morgan, N., & Saxton, J. (1992). *Asking better questions.* Markham, Ontario, Canada: Pembroke.

Murray, D. M. (2002). *Write to learn* (7th ed.). Boston: Heinle.

National Assessment of Educational Progress. (2008). *The nation's report card.* Retrieved April 12, 2008, from http://nces.ed.gov/nationsreportcard/itmrls

National Council of Teachers of English. (2004). *On reading, learning to read, and effective reading instruction: An overview of what we know and how we know it.* Retrieved March 18, 2008, from www.ncte.org/about/over/positions/category/read/118620.htm

National Reading Panel. (2000). *Teaching children to read.* Retrieved March 14, 2008, from http://www.nationalreadingpanel.org/Publications/publications/summary.htm

Nystrand, M., & Gamoran, A. (1991). Instructional discourse, student engagement, and literature achievement. *Research in the Teaching of English, 25*(3), 261–290.

Nystrand, M., Gamoran, A., Kachur, R., & Pendergast, C. (1997). *Opening dialogue: Understanding the dynamics of language and learning in the English classroom.* New York: Teachers College Press.

Nystrand, M., & Weiderspiel, M. (1977). Case study of a personal journal: Notes toward an epistemology of writing. In M. Nystrand (Ed.), *Language as a way of knowing* (pp. 105–121). Toronto, Ontario, Canada: The Ontario Institute for Studies in Education.

Nystrand, M., Wu, L. L., Gamoran, A., Zeiser, S., & Long, D. A. (2003). Questions in time: Investigating the structure and dynamics of unfolding classroom discourse. *Discourse Processes, 35*(2), 135–196.

Olson, C. B., & Land, R. (2007). A cognitive strategies approach to reading and writing instruction for English language learners in secondary school. *Research in the Teaching of English, 41*(3), 269–303.

O'Reilley, M. R. (1998). *Radical presence: Teaching as contemplative practice.* Portsmouth, NH: Heinemann.

O'Reilley, M. R. (2000). *The barn at the end of the world: The apprenticeship of a Quaker, Buddhist shepherd*. Minneapolis, MN: Milkweed Editions.

Palmer, P. (1993). *To know as we are known: Education as a spiritual journey*. San Francisco: HarperCollins.

Palmer, P. (1998). *The courage to teach: Exploring the inner landscape of a teacher's life*. San Francisco: Jossey-Bass.

Palmer, P. (1998/1999). Evoking the spirit in public education. *Educational Leadership, 56*(4), 6–11.

Pert, C. (1997). *Molecules of emotion*. New York: Scribner's.

Pressley, M., & Harris, K. (2001). Teaching cognitive strategies for reading, writing, and problem solving. In A. Costa (Ed.), *Developing minds: A resource book for teaching thinking* (3rd ed., pp. 466–470). Alexandria, VA: Association for Supervision and Curriculum Development.

Ray, K. W. (1999). *Wondrous words: Writers and writing in the elementary classroom*. Urbana, IL: National Council of Teachers of English.

Rider, S. (2003). Tolerating intolerance: Resisting the urge to silence student opinion in the writing classroom. *The Quarterly of the National Writing Project, 25*(1). Retrieved October, 23, 2008, from http://www.nwp.org/cs/public/print/resource/531

Rose, M. (1989). *Lives on the boundary*. New York: Penguin.

Rowe, M. B. (1986, January-February). Wait time: Slowing down may be a way of speeding up! *Journal of Teacher Education*, 43–50.

Sanders, S. R. (1999). Beauty. In E. Hoagland & R. Atwan (Eds.), *The best American essays 1999* (pp. 244–253). Boston: Houghton Mifflin.

Scherer, M. (2005). Required reading. *Educational Leadership, 63*(2), 7.

Schmoker, M. (2006). *Results now*. Alexandria, VA: Association for Supervision and Curriculum Development.

Schmoker, M. (2007). Radically redefining literacy: An immense opportunity. *Phi Delta Kappan, 88*(7), 488–493.

Schoen, D. A. (1987). *Educating the reflective practitioner: Toward a new design for teaching and learning in the professions*. San Francisco: Jossey-Bass.

Schoenbach, R., Greenleaf, C., Cziko, R., & Hurwitz, L. (1999). *Reading for understanding*. San Francisco: Jossey-Bass.

Shapiro, A. (2006). Why write? In L. Slater (Ed.), *The best American essays 2006* (pp. 197–207). New York: Houghton Mifflin.

Shea, M., Murray, R., & Harlin, R. (2005). *Drowning in data?* Portsmouth, NH: Heinemann.

Sizer, T. R., & Sizer, N. F. (1999). *The students are watching us: Schools and the moral contract*. Boston: Beacon Press.

Smith, M., & Wilhelm, J. (2002). *Reading don't fix no Chevies: Literacy in the lives of young men*. Portsmouth, NH: Heinemann.

Snow, C. P. (1998). *The two cultures*. New York: Cambridge University Press.

Sommers, N., & Saltz, L. (2004). The novice as expert: Writing the freshman year. *College Composition and Communication, 56*(1), 124–149.

Sprenger, M. (1999). *Learning & memory: The brain in action*. Alexandria, VA: Association for Supervision and Curriculum Development.

Sprenger, M. (2005). *How to teach so students remember*. Alexandria, VA: Association for Supervision and Curriculum Development.

Sterling, R. (2005). *Common sense and common cause.* Retrieved May 7, 2008, from www.writingproject.org/cs/nwpp/print/nwpr/2278

Suhor, C. (1998/1999). Spirituality—letting it grow in the classroom. *Educational Leadership, 56*(4), 12–16.

Sylwester, R. (1995). *A celebration of neurons: An educator's guide to the human brain.* Alexandria, VA: Association for Supervision and Curriculum Development.

Sylwester, R. (2003). *A biological brain in a cultural classroom* (2nd ed.). Thousand Oaks, CA: Corwin.

Thomas, L. (1978). *The lives of a cell: Notes of a biology watcher.* New York: Penguin.

Tierney, B. (2002). Let's take another look at the fish: The writing process as discovery. In A. Bauman & A. Peterson (Eds.), *Breakthroughs: Classroom discoveries about teaching writing* (pp. 9–17). Berkeley, CA: National Writing Project.

Torbe, M. (1983). Writing about reading. In P. L. Stock (Ed.), *FORUM: Essays on theory and practice in the teaching of writing* (pp. 162–167). Upper Montclair, NJ: Boynton/Cook.

Tovani, C. (2005). The power of purposeful reading. *Educational Leadership, 63*(2), 48–51.

VanDeWeghe, R. (1987, Spring). Making and remaking meaning: Developing literary responses through purposeful, informal writing. *English Quarterly 20*(1), 38–51.

Vygotsky, L. S. (1978). *Mind in society: The development of higher psychological processes.* Cambridge, MA: Harvard University Press.

Williams, S. (1990). Active questions. *Douglas County Higher Literacy Project, 1,* 41–45.

Willis, J. (2006). *Research-based strategies to ignite student learning.* Alexandria, VA: Association for Supervision and Curriculum Development.

Wolfe, P., & Brandt, R. (1998). What do we know from brain research? *Educational Leadership, 56*(3), 8–13.

Wormeli, R. (2004). *Summarization in any subject.* Alexandria, VA: Association for Supervision and Curriculum Development.

Index